BRITISH RULE IN INDIA

BRITISH RULE IN INDIA

SIDDHA MOHANA MITRA
AND
JAMES FERGUSSON

GYAN

Published by

Gyan Publishing House
5, Ansari Road
Daryaganj, New Delhi-110002
Phone: 011-47034999, 9811692060
E-mail: books@gyanbooks.com

Distribution Network
gyanbooks.com
India, USA, Canada, UK, Australia

ISBN: 978-93-6920-206-5 (HB)

First Published, 1905

2nd Impression 2025

Printed at: Gyan Press, Delhi.

BRITISH RULE IN INDIA
Author: SIDDHA MOHANA MITRA and JAMES FERGUSSON

BRITISH RULE IN INDIA

BY

S. M. MITRA, M.R.A.S.

WITH AN INTRODUCTION

BY

THE RIGHT HONOURABLE SIR JAMES FERGUSSON, BART.,
G.C.S.I., K.C.M.G., P.C., LL.D., D.L., J.P., M.P.;
Late Under-Secretary of State, India; Governor of Bombay, etc.

L. ASHBURNER, C.S.I., I.C.S. *retired.*

JOHN POLLEN, C.I.E., LL.D., *Barrister-at-Law*, I.C.S. *retired*,
Lt.-Colonel B.V.R. *retired.*

AND

COLONEL W. LOCH, C.I.E., *Indian Army*, *retired.*

LONDON:
PRINTED BY DALZIEL & CO., LTD.,
CAMDEN PRESS, N.W.

NOTICE.

"BRITISH RULE IN INDIA," by Mr. S. M. MITRA, M.R.A.S., is circulated Free of Cost by the author.

Please apply, enclosing 2½d. stamp, to cover packing and postage, to the undersigned,

F. M. BLAKE,
Stationer, Printer and Bookseller,
92 Haverstock Hill,
London, N.W,

CONTENTS.

PREFACE.

ALTHOUGH these pages are merely a reprint of certain magazine articles I wrote while in India, and although no alterations whatever have been made in the original contributions, this booklet is by no means a bundle of disconnected thoughts. All my contributions to the Indian Press—English, Urdu or Bengali—have been directed to one end, viz., the advancement of the best interests of my native land, by removing friction between the rulers and the ruled. The political opinions expressed in these pages have resulted from prolonged experience of indigenous Indian rule, and from close comparison of the native system of government with the methods adopted by the British Administration. Such a comparison can alone bring out the general problems and difficulties of tropical administration, and by such comparison alone can one really understand the difficulties involved in reconciling the various differences due to caste and traditions of the East, which being transmitted through centuries, have acquired the rigidity of race characteristics. No country in the world can possibly offer a more fascinating field for investigation to the students of politics and sociology than India.

Let no one misunderstand me. I have no wish to disparage my native land. India possesses a great literature and philosophy of her own. In times gone by, she was not only able to manage her own affairs, but actually founded colonies, and rejoiced in oversea expansions. Java, now under the Dutch, was a Hindu colony for over fifteen centuries. India is a vast Continent—the Hindustanis proper outnumber the whites in the United States, the Bengalis are twice as numerous as are the French, and the "fighting castes" in

India number about 125,000,000, or more than the population of the Roman Empire! Neither Greece nor Rome could boast of a third of the number of our King-Emperor's subjects in Asia.

The corner-stone of British policy in India is *Justice*. By a constant unity of purpose, with a government that can boast of great flexibility as well as mechanical precision, the English have been successful with the teeming millions of India, in making them, to a certain extent, think for themselves, and in developing the individuality of the people. The oriental hatred for change is well known. The complexity of interests in India presents difficulties varying in character as well as in magnitude, the solution of which is hard and unromantic work. But the success of the British Indian Administration has been little less than marvellous. Most of the officials work with the precision of machines and the enthusiasm of Crusaders. They have had serious obstacles in their way. The Hindu, indifferent alike to life and comfort, whom even the grand-whip hunger fails to teach much, is separated from the rulers by a gulf of thoughts and aspirations. In the East, thought is stronger than armies.

"The East bowed low before the blast,
In patient deep disdain;
She let the legions thunder past,
Then plunged in thought again."

The so-called critics make the problem of British Administration even more and more difficult. It is a great pity that, with most "critics" on Indian affairs, a sound knowledge of the history of the country is hardly considered essential before the formulation and public utterance of most decided opinions. Nothing in the world is perfect, and I do not for a moment say that the British Administration of India is not capable of great improvements. The rulers show no lack of adjustment to local conditions, though they have yet to teach young India to appreciate the dignity of manual labour. The immense inert mass of peasantry have a firm faith in the "*Sirkar*," and show a willing submissiveness to a strong and consistent government; and not all the harangues of the agitators have as yet been able to influence the current of devotion to the person of the Sovereign and belief in the benignity of his rule. But the profound, possibly unconscious, indifference of English statesmen to Indian affairs, if much longer continued, is likely to break the spell of British prestige in India ; specially as now certain faddists systematically indulge in the luxury of ferreting out isolated instances of injustice, and are trying to shape formless and occasional discontent into a single continuous outcry against imaginary widespread oppression. Sometimes English faddists unwittingly fan the flames of discontent for the mere love of party applause, which has risen among some of them to the height of a passion. With others, it is the hunger for cheap distinction. They have evidently no time to give a thought to the serious nature of their utterances. They forget that modern India is the most striking achievement of the white people in the tropics. The French in Indo-China, the Dutch in Java, or the Americans in the Philippine Islands, have not been half as successful as the English in India.

Therefore, statesmen possessing breadth of view, mental balance, and a tolerant habit of mind, should combine in lifting India above the plane of party bickerings, and should insist on making the sympathetic administration of this great Dependency a duty of national importance and not a mere party cry.

If thoughtful people of this country show their approval of the drift of these papers, and thus stimulate public interest in the vast British Dominions in the East, this booklet will have served a good purpose, and the writer will have been amply rewarded.

June 30th, 1905.

NORTHBROOK SOCIETY,
185 PICCADILLY,
LONDON. W.

S. M. MITRA.

been able to influence the current of devotion to the person of the Sovereign and belief in the benignity of his rule. But the profound, possibly unconscious, indifference of English statesmen to Indian affairs, if much longer continued, is likely to break the spell of British prestige in India ; specially as now certain faddists systematically indulge in the luxury of ferreting out isolated instances of injustice, and are trying to shape formless and occasional discontent into a single continuous outcry against imaginary widespread oppression. Sometimes English faddists unwittingly fan the flames of discontent for the mere love of party applause, which has risen among some of them to the height of a passion. With others, it is the hunger for cheap distinction. They have evidently no time to give a thought to the serious nature of their utterances. They forget that modern India is the most striking achievement of the white people in the tropics. The French in Indo-China, the Dutch in Java, or the Americans in the Philippine Islands, have not been half as successful as the English in India.

Therefore, statesmen possessing breadth of view, mental balance, and a tolerant habit of mind, should combine in lifting India above the plane of party bickerings, and should insist on making the sympathetic administration of this great Dependency a duty of national importance and not a mere party cry.

If thoughtful people of this country show their approval of the drift of these papers, and thus stimulate public interest in the vast British Dominions in the East, this booklet will have served a good purpose, and the writer will have been amply rewarded.

June 30th, 1905.

NORTHBROOK SOCIETY,
185 PICCADILLY,
LONDON. W.

S. M. MITRA.

INTRODUCTION.

Very few people in this country have a clear idea of India. The area of India is about 1,870,000 *square miles, and the population* 300,000,000. *This is equal to the combined population and areas of* 21 *European countries, viz: England, Scotland, Ireland, France, Spain, Portugal, Germany, Austria, Hungary, Belgium, Norway, Sweden, Denmark, Italy, Switzerland, Holland, Turkey, Greece, Roumania, Servia and Bulgaria. Less than* 1,000 *Englishmen are employed in the superior civil government of India. A single Englishman, generally, is responsible for the life and property of about* 300,000 *human beings, and is entrusted with jurisdiction over an area of about* 1,200 *square miles. Such being the case, is it not the duty of every Englishman to know how his countrymen are discharging their sacred trust in*

India? We therefore commend "British Rule in India," by Mr. S. M. Mitra, M.R.A.S., to the notice of our countrymen. Mr. Mitra has been connected with the Indian Press for about twenty years, and for ten years was the proprietor and editor of an English newspaper in India, devoted largely to the affairs of His Highness the Nizam's Dominions. Mr. Mitra's connection with the Premier Native State of India for over fifteen years gave him ample facilities to study an indigenous native government and to compare it with our Indian administration. Therefore he is peculiarly fitted to speak on the subject. The "Graphic" of May 9th, 1903, with an illustration, first introduced Mr. Mitra to the English public as the "generous and enlightened Indian gentleman" who entertained the Indian Mutiny veterans at dinner during Durbar week at Delhi.

Mr. Mitra's articles are written from a frankly appreciative Indian standpoint. The facts and figures which he gives are all taken from Blue Books, Administrative Reports, etc., and show that Mr. Mitra is both a keen observer and a capable critic. His writings, though directed against extreme party exaggerations and misrepresentations, are devoid of any tinge of partiality or one-sidedness. Mr. Mitra displays a grasp of historical facts, and puts before us a distinct aspect of Indian questions, which might be studied with advantage by the "Bleeding India" or "Perish India" school of politicians.

The thoughtful section of his countrymen have evidently taken Mr. Mitra's criticism in good part, for last year the Bengal Academy of Literature, well known in Calcutta as the "Sahitya Parishad," unanimously elected Mr. Mitra to revise the transliteration of all Arabic and Persian words in the Bengali language. Sir William Wedderburn, Bt., and Sir George Birdwood, are Fellows of the "Sahitya Parishad," and the 600 members of this Society—among whom are eminent judges of the Calcutta High Court, members of the

Indian Civil Service, professors, doctors, barristers, etc.—represent the wealth and intellect of Bengal, the foremost province of India. Mr. Mitra is very well connected. He comes from the same stock as the late Raja Digambar Mitra, C.S.I., who in the seventies was a prominent figure in Indian politics, and was in direct touch with more than one Viceroy. Mr. Mitra is also nearly related to the late Maharaja Sir Narendra Krishna Bahadur, K.C.I.E., a well-known member of the aristocracy of Bengal, whose ancestors helped Lord Clive in establishing British Supremacy in India about a hundred and fifty years ago. Mr. B. Dé, M.A., I.C.S., who is now acting as Commissioner of the Burdwan Division in Bengal, and is the third Indian gentleman who has ever held such a high position, is Mr. Mitra's first cousin. Statesmen in this country, who possess clear-sightedness, courage, energy and tact, will readily understand that knowledge, such as the following pages contain, deserves diffusion throughout the land.

Round Famine and Drink circle some of the main controversies of the time. These two subjects are being used as handles for agitation in India and in England. It is therefore with great pleasure we note that in these pages Mr. Mitra has given us historical extracts, in some cases quoting the original Sanskrit and Persian texts, which deal with Famine and Drink in India. Mr. Mitra reached England only a month ago, but he feels that he cannot stand idly by and allow misrepresentations to be spread abroad unchallenged. He has therefore decided to reprint some of his recent magazine articles written in India, and with praiseworthy patriotism ana loyalty proposes circulating his articles on "British Rule in India" FREE OF COST *to all interested therein.*

The time has, we think, now come when the London Press and the leaders of thought in this country should adopt measures towards enlightening the minds of their less well-

informed countrymen with regard to Indian affairs generally. It would be well if Mr. Mitra could be induced to address English audiences on Indian questions, and take other steps to instruct the British Public as to real sentiments of thoughtful and independent natives of India regarding the British administration of that country.

JAMES FERGUSSON.

L. ASHBURNER.

JOHN POLLEN.

WILLIAM LOCH.

June 30th, 1905.

London.

DID ENGLAND TEACH INDIA TO DRINK?

PATRIOTISM no doubt is a virtue, and I should be the last to denounce it or to wish to weaken its hold on my countrymen. But I cannot shut my eyes to what I may call its excesses or its aberrations. Love may be blind. But love of one's country need not be so. A studied indifference to facts, or glossing over one's short-comings, is no patriotism. On the other hand, the true patriot is he who faces facts boldly, however inconvenient and disagreeable they may be. Is it the best way of serving one's country to seek to throw all the blame for the evils that may obtain on others' shoulders? Have we been altogether blameless? That is the question that ought to exercise the minds of all to whom patriotism or public spirit is not merely a cloak to conceal selfish ends. Some of the Indian "patriots," no doubt, are men of erudition. But they do not always seem to recognise that the spirit of exaggeration is neither quite harmless, nor a source of strength. As I pointed out in my article on *Mr. Dutt and Indian Famines,** often a good case is spoilt by even a single exaggerated statement. Indian "patriots" seem to delight in exaggerations, and thus become great favourites of English faddists, who do not pause to consider the incalculable mischief which results from their injudicious speeches and absurd harangues against the Government of India. As it is, the responsible officials of the Government of India have their hands quite full without being made to waste their valuable time in disabusing the minds of their less informed countrymen, of the erroneous

* Page 23.

impressions created by philanthropists, patriots, faddists, *et hoc genus omne.* Take the drink question for example. We all know and readily admit the evils of drink. There is no doubt, that it is the duty of all well-wishers of India to do their best to minimise the evils of drink. But it does not appear to me to be necessary, for this purpose, to try to establish that we were a perfectly sober people before the advent of the British into this country. It would not be honest; besides, truth cannot long be hidden. Long centuries before the British set foot on this soil, long before the Moslem invaders thought of Hindustan, long before Alexander the Great dreamt of the riches of the Gangetic valley, the Indian had been used to the exhilarating effects of drink. The boast is often made, in the columns of newspapers and on public platforms, that we were civilized at a time when some of the foremost nations of to-day were but savages roaming in primeval forests, clothed in beasts' skins and cutting one another's throats. If this is true, it is equally so that while propounding, on the banks of the Ganges, philosophies which still command the admiration of the Western world, we were also indulging in drink as a sort of "religious duty." Wine, "which cheereth gods and men"* was used in India from time immemorial. The most notable case where the sacrificial feast had the use of wine as the chief feature, was the ancient *Sōmarasa* offering of the old Aryans, when the gods were honoured by bowls of precious draught which "heals the sick, inspires the poet, and makes the poor believe that all his wants are satisfied!"

The use of wine is as old as the earliest memory of civilization. In Greece, the introduction of it is ascribed to god Dionysus, and in Egypt to god Osiris. The Hebrews give the credit to Noah—the second father of mankind—while the old Persians say that King Jamshid introduced wine in the Land of Roses. The Old Testament mentions corn and wine as the material basis of life and comfort. Wine was an article of Phœnician commerce. (Ezekiel XXVII. 18.) Wine and olive may be regarded as symbols of settled life in ancient times, for semi-nomadic people did not stay long enough in one spot

* Judges ix. 13.

to form vineyards. Pliny mentions viticulture, but for drink in India we have a much higher authority—I mean the Rig Veda. To satisfactorily prove the existence of indulgence in strong drinks, we have not to refer to works of doubtful authenticity. There exists perhaps no record in the world that carries us back to a more primitive state of the human family than the Rig Veda. It has been very appropriately said that there is no oasis in the vast desert of ancient Asiatic history as the Rig Veda, the earliest existing literary record of the Aryan race.* The Rig Veda being the earliest history of the Aryan race, is justly called the historical Veda by Professor Roth and other Western *savants*. It is very difficult to fix the age of the Vedas, and even such profound Oriental scholars as Professor Max Müller and Dr. Haug have failed to fix milestones in Vedic literature. All scholars disagree. One tries to measure by the revolution of the heavenly bodies, another by the progress of the human mind. The hymns of the Vedas were, it is said, collected and arranged by Krishna Dvaipāyana Vyāsa.† According to Bentley and Archdeacon Pratt, the date of the compilation is 1181 B.C. Max Müller says that the Rig Veda was composed about a thousand years before Christ, Sir William Jones and Colebrooke assign fifteen hundred years before Christ; while Dr. Haug fixed the Vedic literature 2400 B.C.‡ It is the worshippers of the Devas—the Hindu Aryans—who have composed these hymns, writes Mr. Dutt, which are known as the Rig Veda. Probably there is not another work in the literature of mankind which is so deeply interesting, so unique in the lessons it imparts. The hoary antiquity of this ancient work, the picture it affords of the earliest form of civilization that the Aryans developed in any part of the world, and the flood of light it throws on the origin of the myths and religions of all Aryan nations, make the Rig Veda deeply interesting. It explains how the mind of man in its infancy worships what is bright and glorious in nature,

* Max Müller's *Chips from a German Workshop*, I, p. 5. Roth's *Literature and History of the Vedas*, p. 13.

† Lassen's *Indian Antiquities*, I, p. 777.

‡ Haug's *Aitareya—Brahmana*, I, p. 47, and Weber's *History of Indian Literature*.

what is powerful and striking. Among less happy nations religion began with the dread of diseases and of evils, as these made the most lasting impression on the mind. *It is the oldest work in the Aryan world.** Whatever the exact date may be, the Rig Veda is, as everyone admits, the oldest history of the Aryan race. Its contents have always attracted the highest reverence and admiration.† In the Rig Veda there is ample evidence, that from the earliest Vedic period the people of India indulged in drink. *Sōmarasa* was their favourite beverage. They worshipped it! Without the *Soma* (Asclepias-acida) two important religious ceremonies (Yajnas) called *Shautramani* and *Bājpeya* could not be performed. The *Soma* was from the earliest times connected with the religious history of the Indo-Aryans.‡ The antiquity of the cultus is attested by the references which are made to it in the Zend Avesta. The coincidence between the Vedic *Agnishtoma*, and the *Haoma* ceremony of the followers of Zoroaster, testify to the complete development of the *Soma* ritual before the separation of the Indo-Aryans.¶

The *Soma* plant was worshipped as a deity, and one entire *mandala* (lit. circle, chapter) of the *Rig Veda* is dedicated to it; and the principal object for which the *Sāma Veda* was composed was the performance of the sacrifices in which *Sōmarasa* was chiefly required. The exhilarating and inebriating effects of the *Soma* liquor are frequently referred to in the *Rig Veda*. Indra (the great god) drank it to such excess that his stomach used occasionally to get distended! In one of the hymns of the Rig Veda it is mentioned that "the praiseworthy *Soma* has from ancient times been the drink of the gods; he was milked from the hidden recesses of the sky; he was created for Indra and was extolled." Again *Soma* is thus invoked;—"O *Soma!* there is nothing so bright as thou.

---

* Dutt's *Civilization in Ancient India.*

† Whitney's *Oriental and Linguistic Studies*, p. 22.

‡ Windischmann's *Dissertations on the Soma worship of the Arians;* Lassen's *Indian Antiquities*, I, p. 516; and Roth's articles in the Journal of the German Oriental Society for 1848 (p. 216 ff.) and 1850 (p. 417 ff.).

¶ Plutarch de Isid et Osir 46, in which the *Soma* or as it is in Zend *Haoma* appears to be referred.

When poured, thou welcomest all the gods to bestow on them immortality." * The Vedic Aryans gradually found that the mild *Soma juice* did not satisfy them, so they introduced fermentation. No apostle of temperance dare try to show that *Sōmarasa* was not a strong wine. The *Sōmarasa*, though literally the *juice* of the *Soma* plant, was by no means the juice in its natural state. The drink known as *Sōmarasa* was carefully manufactured. In all the four Vedas, many *mantras* (incantations) are given to be used at every stage of its manufacture. The plants were gathered by the roots on the hills on a moonlight night, and after being stripped of their leaves they were carried by rams to the house of the priests. The stalks were then deposited in the hall of oblation, and bruised and crushed between stones and placed with the juice in a sieve of goat's hair, and were further pressed and squeezed with the priest's ten fingers, one or two of which being ornamented with rings of flattened gold. Finally the juice, mixed with barley, wheat, and *ghee* (clarified butter), *was allowed to ferment*. It was then drawn off in a scoop called *sruch*. The gods had this beverage three times a day and the priests helped themselves with ladlefuls just before offering to the gods. The turn of the ordinary mortal came after the priests. The juice of the *Soma* creeper itself possessed no narcotic property or its keeping quality; but being allowed to ferment with barley or *nivara* (wild paddy) in a jar for nine days, it acquired its inebriating effect. It was preserved in bags of cow-skin, rendered impervious by oil or resinous substances. †

Mr. R. C. Dutt, C. I. E., in his *Civilization in Ancient India*, says :—The process by which the *Soma juice* was prepared has been fully described in IX., 66, and in other hymns :—"7. O *Soma!* you have been crushed, you flow as a stream to Indra, scattering joy on all sides; you bestow immortal food. 8. Seven women stir thee with their fingers, blending their voices in a song to thee, you remind the sacrificer of his duties at the sacrifice. 9. You mix with water with a pleasing sound and the fingers stir you over a woollen strainer, and filter you.

* Rig Veda, IX, 110, 8, 108, 3.

† Stevenson's Sama Veda, Haug's Aitareya Brahmana, I, p. 6, and Rig Veda, V. 5, 19.

Your particles are thrown up then, and a sound arises from the woollen strainer. 11. The woollen strainer is placed on a vessel and the fingers repeatedly stir the *Soma*, which sends down a sweet stream into the vessel. 13. O *Soma!* you are then mixed with milk. Water runs towards thee with a pleasing sound."

The reference to cow-skin bags need not startle the "religious" Hindu of the twentieth century. I am referring to our forefathers, centuries before the Christian era, when bulls, rams, and buffaloes formed a portion of Hindu food. I am referring to that period of Hindu history when the term "beef-eater" was not an abuse, on the other hand, when a guest was called a cow-killer (*goghna*), for in his honour the hospitable Hindu matron always killed a cow. The guest in those days was entitled to *Madhuparka* (honeyed meal) and beef. Mr. Dutt says that animal food was largely used by the early Hindus. We have frequent allusions to the sacrifice and to the cooking of cows, buffaloes, and bulls (I. 61, 12; II. 7, 5; V. 29, 7 and 8; VI. 17, 11; VI. 16, 47; VI. 28, 4; X. 27, 2; X. 28, 3, etc.). In X. 89, 14 there is mention of a slaughter-house where cows were killed, and in X. 91, 14 there is an allusion to the sacrifice of horses, bulls and rams. A fairly complete account of the sacrifice of the horses, such as it prevailed in the Vedic times, is to found in hymn 162 of the first Mandala of the Rig Veda. The body of the horse was marked with a cane and was then dissected along the lines marked, and the ribs and the different limbs were separated. The meat was roasted and boiled, while the soul of the horse was supposed to go to the gods!* Mr. Dutt says that a *Brahmanā* lays down instructions for carving beef, and the Gopatha Brahmanā tells us who received the different portions. The priest got the tongue, the neck, the shoulder, the rump, the legs, etc., while the master of the house (wisely) appropriated to himself the sirloin, and his wife had to content herself with the pelvis! *Plentiful libations of the Soma beer were taken to wash down the meat!* In III. 1, 2, 21 of the *Satapatha Brahmanā* there is an amusing discussion, says Mr. Dutt, as to the propriety of eating the meat of an ox or

* Dutt's *Civilization in Ancient India*, p. 41.

cow. The conclusion is not very definite. "Let him (the priest) not eat the flesh of a cow and the ox." Nevertheless Yajnavalkya said (taking apparently a very practical view of the matter), "I for one eat it, *provided it is tender!*" Beef was cooked in *Kapala* and broth kept in *Kalasa*. These were earthen pots. In the primitive state of Hindu civilization cow's skin was largely used for making vessels and bottles.*

But let us return to our subject. In the Rig Veda † reference is often made to swillers of wine. Besides *Soma*, there were in ancient India other strong drinks which were publicly sold in the shops, without practically any reserve, to all comers. Gradually, when drink became the national vice, law makers began to denounce it. We now come to the *Sruti* and the *Smriti*. The *Sruti* means revelation and includes *Mantras*, *Brahmanas*, *Aryanakas* (B.C. 1300), and *Upanishads* (B.C. 1100), —originally the act of sitting down near a teacher and submissively listening to him.‡ The *Smriti* means recollections and includes *Vedangas* and *Sutras*. The *Smriti* also includes, says Mr. Dutt, works composed by holy personages, the *Dharma Shastras* and the *Dharma Sutras* of the Rationalistic Period comprising the institutes of civil and religious law. The distinction between the *Sruti* and the *Smriti* was established prior to the rise of Buddhism. The *Smriti* has no claim to an independent authority, but derives its sanction from its relation to the *Sruti*. In the *Sruti* and the *Smriti* drinking was made penal as the killing of a Brahman, for which capital punishment was awarded. But gradually the Brahman began to lose his supreme authority, and several centuries before the advent of Buddha, Vishvamitra of the royal caste (Kshatriya) refused to submit to the hierarchical pretentions of the Brahman, and succeeded in making the proud priest reasonable and obtained certain privileges. He was followed by King Janaka of Videha in questioning Brahman authority. Gradually when the religion of the Brahman degenerated and the Brahmanas

* Rig Veda, III, 45, 4.

† Rig Veda, III, 45, 1.

‡ Muller's *History of Ancient Sanskrit Literature*, p. 319.

were unable to distinguish themselves in theological discussions, Sakya Muni in the sixth century B.C. entered the field of religious investigation, and the people accepted Buddhism as a tolerant and comprehensive religion. Crusade against drink was one of the ten stern commandments of the great Buddha. He preached :—"The householder who delights in the law should not indulge in *intoxicating drinks*, should not cause others to drink, should not sanction the acts of those who drink, knowing that it results in insanity. The ignorant commit sins in consequence of drunkenness and also make others to drink. You should avoid this : it is the cause of demerit, insanity and ignorance—though it be pleasing to the ignorant."* Drinking of spirituous liquors was termed *Mahapataka* (heinous sin) by Manu. According to *Manu Sanhita*† the expiation for a Brahman guilty of drinking was suicide by a draught of boiling hot spirit, water, milk or cow's urine taken in a burning hot metal pot. Another expiatory prescription was a draught of molten silver, copper or lead. The great Hindu Legislator Manu enjoined that the drunkard Brahman was to be branded on his forehead with the mark of a "vintner's flag," to proclaim that he was an outcast. But latterly the great Manu found that stopping drink was impossible and he was obliged to wink at it. Nay, the great Lawgiver being afraid to denounce it, actually ruled :—"*Na mansa bhakshané dosho na madyé*," *i.e.*, there is no harm in eating meat or in drinking wine !

The Hindus, like the Greeks, possess two great national epics, the *Ramayana* and the *Mahabharata*. The Ramayana of Valmiki consists of 24,000 *slokas* or 48,000 lines of 16 syllables and is divided into seven volumes. Whether we accept Dr. A. Holtzmann's views, that the principal features of the *Mahabharata* go back to Indo-Germanic times, or we agree with Lassen, it must be admitted that it is certain that it is an *old* epic, for Dion Chrysostom (80 A.D.) refers to it. According to Mr. Dutt, B.C. 1250 is the date of Kuru-Panchala war, the subject of the Mahabharata. The work consists of 100,000

* *Buddhism*, by Professor Rhys Davids, pp. 138 and 139.

† (IX, pp. 91-96).

couplets or about eight times the bulk of Homer's Iliad and Odyssey combined. The *Mahabharata* and the *Ramayana* in their present shape are productions of a later age—or rather of later ages—and in their present forms, the incidents of the wars described are undoubtedly mythical, as the incidents described in the Iliad are mythical. The five Pandava brothers and their common wife are myths, as Achilles and Paris and Helen are myths. The *Mahabharata* received its last touches in the Pauranic Age. Though utterly valueless as a narrative of historical events, yet these epics, Mr. Dutt says, *faithfully describe the manners and customs of the ancient Hindus*, as the Iliad describes the manners of the ancient Greeks. *

In the *Adiparva* of the *Mahabharata* we find wine flowing like water in Arjuna's feast on the Raivatak hill. Krishna and Arjuna looked drunk, the Sanskrit words are *madirayat netra* (drunken eyes). Even Hindu ladies were no teetotalers. In *Mahabharata* we read Súdeshna, queen of Virāta, sending her maid Draupadi to Kichak to procure liquor. Liquor was responsible for the Yadavas not recognising the enemy in the battle-field, and killing each other instead; for we read :—*Bárunin madiram pītva madon-mathita cheta-sam, etc.* Now let us take the other epic—the *Ramayana*. The blue ribbon was not the order of the day. Even great saints (rishis) entertained each other with wines. We find the great Vasistha offering wine to his colleague (rival ?) Vishvamitra. Both were honoured by the great King Sudas. When King Bharata, brother of Rama, visited the great saint Bharadvaj, the escort of the King was entertained by the saint with liquor. The Jataka if full of anecdotes of drunkards. Among Sanskrit authors Kalidasa (A.D. 500) perhaps occupies the highest place. He refers more than once to friends offering wine. Mr. Dutt says :—"We know from Sakuntala that there were grogshops which were frequented by the very lowest castes; while among courtiers of a luxurious court, and among the profligate and the gay, drinking was not unknown. Bharavi (A.D. 550) has a canto on the joys of drinking, and Kalidasa, too, *often speaks of ladies whose mouths were scented with the perfumes of liquor!!!*"

* Dutt's *Civilization in Ancient India*, pp. 123, 138.

In *Raghuvansa* in the 9th Canto Maharaja Aja in his lamentations refers to his sweetheart's manner of taking wine.

In *Mārkandeya Chandi* goddess Durga thus addresses Asura :—

"*Tishtha tishtha kshanam mudha madhuyabat piba myaham,*" *i.e.*, just wait you idiot till I finish my drink. Hinduism now in vogue for the last thirteen hundred years in India, is generally based on the *Tantras.* The *Tantric* doctrine has practically usurped the place of the Vedic creed. The very Vedic *mantras* (incantations) have, in a way, filtered through the *Tantras.* In some ceremonies wine is indispensably necessary. In the *Matrikabheda Tantra*, Mahadeva (the great god) takes his wife goddess Parvati into his confidence and says :— "*Brahmanasya mahamoksham madyapāné priyamvadé*, *i.e.*, great salvation of Brahman depends on drinking wine, O my darling. In another place we read:—*Madyapanam vina devi tatva jnanam nalabhyate,*" *i.e.*, without drink, O goddess, you cannot understand religion. "*Ataebahi biprastu madyapānam samācharet,*" therefore a Brahman should drink wine.*

Drink was not confined to the Aryans. The contagion spread and the aborigines developed a taste for liquor. Nay, they actually became drunkards. Let us take the Kols, the aborigines of Bengal. While sober they evidently cannot worship the Deity. To secure salvation they chant :—"*Pītva pītva punah pītva, punah patati bhutale; Utthayacha punah pītva punarjanma navidyate,*" *i.e.*, "Drink, drink, drink again, again fall down on the ground and get up, again drink and *you shall not be born again.*" Even at the present day, the *Tantric Yogini* (female devotee) indulges in wine. But instead of an earthen pot, she uses a human skull as her wine glass. More instances may be quoted from Sanskrit authors to show that drink was the prevailing vice among ancient Hindus, but the above extracts ought to suffice.

We now come to India under Moslem rule. Was drink unknown then ? We all know that wine of every kind is *strictly* forbidden by the Prophet of Arabia. Muslim law makes no

* Dr. R. L. Mitra's *Indo-Aryans*, Vol. I, page 408.

distinction between a drunkard and a temperate wine drinker. If two witnesses testify that a Musalman drank wine, or his breath smells of wine, the punishment is eighty stripes.* But had all this much effect on the Musalman who could afford the luxury? Moslem historians bear testimony to the effect that India under the followers of the Prophet, instead of abolishing the forbidden drink, actually under Royal patronage improved it to make it acceptable to palates used to the delicate wines of Shiraz. Scores of historians may be quoted in support of this statement, but I shall refer to only some of those that enjoy more or less a European reputation. *Tarikh-us-Sabaktgin*, otherwise known as *Tarikh-i-Baihaki'* by Khwaja Abul Fazl bin Al Hasan Baihaki, is a well-known history. According to Khāki Shirāzi, Baihaki died in 1077 A.D. *Tarikh-i-Baihaki* is referred to in Haji Khalifa's lexicon. Meer Khond, in the preface to his world-renowned work, *Rauzat-us-Safā*, says that it contains 30 volumes and that is why it is sometimes called *Mujalladat-i-Baihaki* or volumes of Baihaki. The great Ferishta and Barni have accepted it as authentic history. Akbar's Minister, Abul Fazl Allami, refers to it in his *Ayin-i-Akbari*. In *Tarikh-us-Sabaktgin* we find that Muhammad left Ali Ariyaruk as Governor of the Punjab. The King sent him fifty flagons of wine. Baihaki says that in those days not only the soldiers and officers indulged in drunken brawls, but the Sultan Masud himself used to enjoy regular bouts in which he triumphantly saw all his fellow-topers. We read that one of the courtiers easily finished five tankards—each held nearly a pint of wine—but the sixth confused him, the seventh bereft him of his senses, and at the eighth he was consigned to his servants. Everyone rolled or was rolled away!! The actual Persian words are *Chūn gūyi shūdah*, *i.e.*, having become cricket balls! Again we find in *Tarikh-us-Sabaktgin*, that in November, 1034, just about Muharram, the Sultan fell ill on the banks of Jhelam (Punjab), and in a fit of repentance renounced wine, and the royal cellar was emptied into the river (Jhelam), but this pious resolution did not last long, for we read that the following New Year day was celebrated with great *éclat*—a drinking bout was also held.

* *Hidaya* and *Mishkat*, *Khamr*.

Jami-ul-Hikāyāt of Maulana Nuruddin Muhammad Ufi is known to Western scholars. Professor John Dowson says that it bears much the same relation to the History of India as "*Memorabilia of Velerius Maximus*" bear to the History of Rome. The author's residence at Delhi under Altamsh in 1211 A.D. gave him facilities for carefully sifting his material which he collected from *Tarikh Yamini, Tarikh Nasiri, Tarikh-ul-Abbas, Sharfun-Nabi,* and *Akhbar-i-Baramika,* etc. Haji Khalifa has referred to *Jami-ul-Hikayat* and a Turkish version is referred to by Hammer Purgstall. Ufi refers to Sultan Mahmud and his courtiers drinking wine and enjoying themselves. *Tarikh-i-Firuz-Shahi* of Ziauddin Barni is the chief source from which the great Ferishta draws his account of the period. Barni says that Sultan Balban was for some time addicted to drink. His example spread and everyone acquired a taste for drink. In time, the thirst for wine became insatiable and drink was responsible for acts which in sober moments seemed impossible. Barni refers to an instance when a wily courtier took advantage of a King's drunkenness to obtain the sanction for the murder of a prince! Under royal patronage wines improved. Barni says that the wines which Firuz Shah used to drink were of various colours and of different flavours, some were yellow as saffron, some red as rose, while others were white. It appears that in the case of Indian wines no acquired taste was necessary, for the taste of all was like sweet milk. Occasionally a Musalman *Dervish* or Maulavi appeared on the scene and lectured the King on the evils of drink, reciting the holy writs of Islam, advised the King to give up wine. The result was that for a time reaction set in, and the King put wine drinkers and wine sellers in pits and turned out vintners from the city, but found it impossible to wholly suppress the use of wine, and was obliged to wink at a certain amount of drinking till he or his successor re-opened the wine shops and all the world drank.

Tuzak-i-Babari, the autobiography of Babar, was originally written in Turkish. It is well known to English readers by the admirable translations of Dr. Leyden and Mr. Erskine. "Babar's memoirs," says Professor John Dowson, M.R.A.S., "form one of the best and most faithful pieces of autobiography extant; they are infinitely superior to the hypocritical revelations of Timur, and the pompous declamation of Jehangir—not inferior in any respect to the Expedition of Xenophon and rank but little below the *Commentaries of Cæsar*." Babar entered India in 1526 A.D. In his autobiography he makes the following edifying remark, "as at forty I intend to give up drink (and I am now 39), I am drinking hard!" But at forty the pious resolution was not carried out. When he was defeated by the Rajpúts at Sikri (now Fatehpur-Sikri) and was told that drink was the cause of his defeat, he renounced wine and broke his drinking cups. Akbar's reign is considered the brightest period of Moslem rule in India. Volumes have been written showing Akbar's reforms and the *Ayin-i-Akbari* may be regarded as an authentic record of Akbar's reign. In Akbar's time, wine was allowed to be publicly sold. Akbar himself indulged in wine. In *Ayin-i-Akbari* we read: "When His Majesty is inclined to drink wine, trays of fruit are set before him." The word used by Persian writers is *sharab* which literally means drink, but commonly used to mean wines and spirits.

Tarikh-i-Salim Shahi is another Persian history known to the Western world. It was translated into English by Major David Price for the Oriental Translation Committee under the title of *Memoirs of Jehangir.* There is another translation by Mr. Jones Anderson, published in the Asiatic Miscellany printed at Calcutta in 1785. The difference between these versions has been marked by M. De Sacy in the *Journal-de-Savans*, 1830. Jahangir was as fond of liquor as his great-grandfather Babar, and drinking bouts were very common. It is notorious that Jahangir's brothers, Murad and Dāniyāl, both died of drink. Jahangir was so much addicted to drink that he made no secret of it. He is the only Moslem Monarch in the world who enjoyed the unique distinction of having, with unblushing effrontery, his image—*wine cup in hand, stamped on his gold coins! Waqiat-i-Jahangiri* is known to the Western world. "*Reign of Jehangir*," by Gladwin, published in 1788, is an extract from this work. In this work

Jahangir frankly tells us how much liquor he used to consume every day. He sometimes took twenty cups of double distilled liquor, and each cup contained seven tolas of wine. Therefore twenty cups means 140 tolas.*

We have quoted Hindu and Musalman authors. Now let us give a few extracts from the writings of disinterested travellers. We will only refer to those who saw things with their own eyes and published *bonâ fide* accounts of their travels before the days of faddists and missionaries.

Megasthenes, says Mr. Dutt, came to India in the fourth century before Christ, and lived in the court of Chandragupta in Pataliputra or ancient Patna. Although his original account is lost, still extracts from his writings are found scattered in many subsequent woıks. These have been carefully collected by Dr. Schwanbeck, of Bonn, and translated into English by Dr. MacCrindle, and are invaluable for the purposes of Indian History. Pythagoras, Herodotus and Megasthenes are unimpeachable witnesses to the high civilization of India during three successive centuries which fall within the Rationalistic Period, *viz.*, the sixth, fifth and fourth centuries before Christ.† Megasthenes thus refers to the use of wine at sacrifices. "The Hindu beverage is a liquor composed from rice instead of barley."

François Bernier's *Travels in the Moghul Empire*, 1656-1668 A.D., is a well-known work. He does not deny the existence of wine in India. He drank some wine at Ahmedabad (Bombay) and Golkonda. The good wine he found in the Moghul Empire was sent by land from Persia to Bandar Abbas, where it embarked for Surat, from which port it reached Delhi in 46 days. Another kind of wine was imported by the Dutch. He says that these wines taken in moderation were found excellent preservatives against malaria. The liquor peculiar to the country was called *arak*, a spirit drawn from unrefined sugar, and was harsh and burning as that made of corn in Poland. Bernier, of course, mentions that none but Christians

---

* 2½ tolas = one ounce.

† Dutt's *Civilization in Ancient India*, p. 211.

did *openly* drink in those days. Bernier evidently did not come across Jahangir's gold coins. There was another kind of wine called *Bouleponge,* a drink composed of *arak* mixed with lemon juice, water and nutmeg. *Boule* is the German name for punch and allied drinks. The Bengal *arak* was held in great repute in those days. Ovington* says: "Bengal *arak* is much stronger than that of *Goa* and both are made use of by Europeans in making punch."

Jean Baptiste Tavernier was perhaps the most renowned traveller of the seventeenth century. In his *Travels* he refers to wine at Lahore (Punjab). Most likely he would have found wine elsewhere too; but as the great traveller carried his own French wines with him, to which he makes frequent reference, he did not take the trouble to find out, or finding the native *arak* harsh to the French palate, he did not condescend to refer to it. Probably the Lahore vintners satisfied the great traveller, and hence prominence is given to Lahore wine.

We may also refer to Captain Hawkins who was with Jahangir from 1608 to 1613. He has described at great length Jahangir's drinking habits.† With one or two quotations from official records we shall finish this article. In Wheeler's *Early Records of British India* is published *in extenso* a letter written by the Rev. Patrick Warner, dated 31st January, 1676:

"It may be for a lamentation to hear and see the horrid swearing and profanation of the name of God, the *woful and abominable drunkenness* and uncleanness that so much reign and rage among the soldiery; and these not secretly or covertly but as it were in the sight of the sun, and men refuse therein to be ashamed; neither can they blush." In the *Early Records of British India* importation of wines from Persia is mentioned more than once. The following is taken from Captain Hamilton's accounts:—"Captain Perrin, master of a ship, brought in Bengal good ship-store of Persian wines .... Two gentlemen of the council being that season bound for England, coming one day to dine with me I treated them and

* A voyage to Surat in the year 1686, London, 1696.

† Hawkins' Voyages by Markham, Hakluyt Society, 1878.

the rest of my company with that Persian wine which they all praised and asked me where I got it from. I told them knowing that good wines would be scarce that year, I had provided a good quantity at Surat from whence I had come that season. Everyone begged that I would spare them some chests which I condescended to do as a favour; and next day sent them what they wanted at double the price the owner demanded for it, and so got off above a hundred and twenty chests which enabled Mr. Perrin to satisfy most of his creditors."

So we have now quotations from both sacred and secular Sanskrit literature in support of drink in the Hindu period. Though the Koran *strictly* prohibits the use of wine, we have the unsolicited testimony of Moslem historians to say that not only wine was used, but was actually abused during the Muhammadan period of Indian History. If further evidence was wanted we have quoted the three foreign travellers and an Englishman, who actually lived with Jahangir, and who, when writing his account, had not dreamt that his countrymen would be the conquerors of India. It is now clear that Indians from time immemorial, brewed their own wine, used it always, abused it occasionally, and imported it from Persia, whenever they could afford the luxury—*England did not teach India to drink.**

---

* The *Calcutta Review*, October, 1904.

MR. DUTT AND INDIAN FAMINES.

THE subject of Indian Famines, pregnant as it is with deep and vital importance, is drawing a good deal of attention, both in England and in India. In most cases the writings on the subject are characterised by an ardent desire to ameliorate the condition of the Indian ryot. For some time, the letters and articles with reference to famine which appeared in the public press passed practically unnoticed, at least officially; but when on the 20th December, 1900, the following petition was presented to the Secretary of State by no less than eleven retired Indian officials of high rank, it drew official attention, and their utterances carried weight as much from the past position of the signatories as from the moderate language in which the petition was couched :—

(1) "In view of the terrible famines with which India has been lately afflicted, we the undersigned who have spent many years of our lives among the people, and still take a deep interest in their welfare, beg to offer the following suggestions to your Lordship in Council, in the hope that the Land Revenue Administration may be elsewhere placed on such a sound and equitable basis as to secure to the cultivators of the soil a sufficient margin of profit to enable them better to withstand the pressure of future famine.

(2) "We are well aware that the primary cause of famines is the failure of rain, and that the protection of large tracts of country by the extension of irrigation from sources that seldom or never fail has been steadily kept in view and acted on by the Government for many years past; but the bulk of the

country is dependent on direct rain fall, and the pinch of famine is most severely felt in the uplands, where the crops fail simply for want of rain. The only hope for the cultivators throughout the greater part of India is, therefore, that they should be put in such a position as to enable them to tide over an occasional bad season.

(3) "To place the cultivators in such a position we consider it essential that the share taken as the Government demand on the land should be strictly limited in every Province. We fully agree with the views of Lord Salisbury, when Secretary of State for India, as set out in his minute of 26th of April, 1875 :—

'So far as it is possible to change the Indian fiscal system, it is desirable that the cultivator should pay a smaller portion of the whole national charge. It is not in itself a thrifty policy to draw the mass of revenue from the rural districts where capital is scarce, sparing the towns, where it is often redundant and runs to waste and luxury. The injury is exaggerated in the case of India, where so much of the revenue is exported without a direct equivalent.'

(4) "Without going into tedious details, we consider it very advisable that in those parts of the country in which the Land Tax is not permanently settled the following principles should be uniformly adhered to :—

(*a*) "Where the Land Revenue is paid directly by the cultivators, as in most parts of Madras and Bombay, the Government demand should be limited to 50 per cent. of the value of the net produce after a liberal deduction for cultivation expenses has been made, and should not ordinarily exceed one-fifth of the gross produce, even in those parts of the country where, in theory, one-half of the net is assumed to appropriate to one-third of the gross produce.

(*b*) "Where the Land Revenue is paid by landlords, the principle adopted in the Saharanpur Rules of 1855, whereby the Revenue demand is limited to one-half of the actual rent or assets of such landlords, should be universally applied.

(*c*) "That no revision of the Land Tax of any Province or part thereof should be made within thirty years of the expiration of any former revision.

(*d*) "That when such revision is made in any of those parts of India where the Land Revenue is paid by the cultivators direct to the Government there should be no increase in the assessment except in cases where the land has increased in value (1) in consequence of improvements in irrigation works carried out at the expense of the Government or (2) on account of a rise in the value of produce based on the average prices of the thirty years next preceding such revision.

(5) "Lastly, we recommend that a limit be fixed in each Province beyond which it may not be permissible to surcharge the Land Tax with local cesses. We are of opinion that the Bengal rate of 6¼ per cent. is a fair one, and that in no case should the rate exceed 10 per cent.

(Sd.) R. K. BUCKLE,
Late Director of Revenue Settlement and Member of the Board of Revenue, Madras.

" J. H. GARSTIN,
Late Member of Council, Madras.

" J. B. PENNINGTON,
Late Collector of Tanjore, Madras.

" H. J. REYNOLDS,
Late Revenue Secretary to the Government of Bengal and late Member of the Legislative Council of the Governor-General of India.

" RICHARD GARTH,
Late Chief Justice of Bengal.

" ROMESCH C. DUTT,
Late Officiating Commissioner of Orissa Division in Bengal, and Member of the Bengal Legislative Council.

(Sd.) C. J. O'DONNELL,

Late Commissioner of Bhagalpore and Rajshahi Divisions in Bengal.

" A. ROGERS,

Late Settlement Officer and Member of Council in Bombay.

" W. WEDDERBURN,

Late Acting Chief Secretary to the Government of Bombay.

" JOHN JARDINE,

Late Judge of the High Court, Bombay.

" J. P. GOODRIDGE,

Late B. C. S., and formerly Officiating Settlement Commissioner, Central Provinces.

Among the signatories Mr. R. C. Dutt, C.I.E. (I.C.S. Retired), late Officiating Commissioner of Orissa and Member of the Bengal Legislative Council, returned to the charge in India and carried on an active campaign in a series of open letters addressed to the Viceroy. Mr. Dutt is not an antagonist to be despised. Added to the glamour of his name as oriental scholar and historian, the author of some works on ancient India, there is the stern fact that he is a Revenue Officer of great experience. Lord Curzon's Government welcomed the opportunity thus afforded of discussing a question which is one of the highest national importance. Mr. Dutt's open letters were, therefore, referred to all Local Governments for their consideration and report, and from the mass of information received from various Provinces, Lord Curzon was able to issue Resolution of the 16th January, 1902, which is a comprehensive review of Land Revenue policy throughout India. In that Resolution His Excellency claimed to have established the following points :—

(1) That a permanent Settlement, whether in Bengal or elsewhere, is no protection against the incidence and consequences of famine ;

(2) That in areas where the State receives its land revenue from landlords, progressive moderations is the keynote of the policy of Government, and that the standard of 50 per cent. of the assets is one which is more often departed from on the side of the deficiency than of excess;

(3) That in the same area the State has not and does not hesitate to interfere by legislation to protect the interests of the tenants against oppression at the hands of the landlords;

(4) That in areas where the State takes the land revenue from the cultivators, the proposal to fix assessment at one-fifth of the gross produce would result in the imposition of a greatly increased burden upon the people;

(5) That the policy of long term settlement is gradually being extended, the exceptions being justified by conditions of local development;

(6) That a simplification and cheapening of the proceedings connected with new settlements and an avoidance of the harassing invasion of an army of subordinate officials are a part of the deliberate policy of Government;

(7) That the principle of exempting or allowing for improvements is one of general acceptance but may be capable of further extension;

(8) That assessments have ceased to be made upon prospective assets;

(9) That local taxation as a whole, though susceptible of some redistribution, is neither immoderate nor burdensome;

(10) That over-assessment is not as alleged, a general or widespread source of poverty and indebtedness in India, and that it cannot fairly be regarded as a contributory cause of famine;

The Government of India have further laid down liberal principles for future guidance, and will be prepared, where the necessity is established, to make further advance in respect of:—

(11) The progressive and graduated imposition of large enhancements;

(12) Greater elasticity in the revenue collection facilitating its adjustment to the variations of the seasons and the circumstances of the people;

(13) A more general resort of reduction of assessments in cases of local deterioration where such reduction cannot be claimed under the terms of settlement.

The conclusions arrived at by Lord Curzon's Government were not, however, satisfactory to Mr. Dutt, and several letters appeared in the *Pioneer* and other journals over the signature of Mr. Dutt, in *reply* to the Government Resolution. As far as I am aware, no Indian has had the courage to question in any public print the correctness of Mr. Dutt's dictum, and yet there must be some among the educated classes who know and feel that they cannot endorse all that he has said. It may have been a mistaken idea of what patriotism really is, which prompted silence in the presence of a great leader of Congress thought, or was it a natural disinclination to cross swords with so doughty an opponent? The fact remains that Mr. Dutt's statements—some of which are hardly calculated to gain for Mr. Dutt the reputation of a reliable historian—have either been endorsed or allowed to pass unchallenged. Let me give an instance. Mr. Dutt says "the famines which have desolated India within the last quarter of the 19th century *are unexampled in their extent and intensity in the history of ancient or modern times.*"

The italics are mine. The sentence I have quoted is not one hurriedly dashed off for the columns of a newspaper. It will be found in Mr. Dutt's "*Economic History of British India*" published in England last year. The assertion is a sweeping one, and any thoughtful man may be pardoned, if, after wading through Mr. Dutt's writings on the subject, he is forced to exclaim "not proven." Even the Government of India's exhaustive Resolution on the subject does not challenge this statement, and perhaps therefore Mr. S. N. Bannerji in his Presidential address at the last (1902) Congress asserts that the Viceroy himself says that the last famine of the last quarter of the expiring century was *the severest that the country has ever known.* (*Vide* Mr. Bannerji's speech, Press copy, last line, page 21). It may, therefore, seem temerity in me to venture into the arena; but if I am able to disprove fallacies, I may perchance render some little aid to the great work of devising means of occupying philanthropists, patriots and faddists, by asking them to relinquish untenable ground, and renew their researches into avenues where their efforts will be rewarded with more tangible results than has attended such sweeping criticism, unsupported by facts and figures, of the acts and intentions of a Government that commands the respect of the civilized world. Mr. Dutt himself will perhaps admit that often a good case is spoilt by even one unreliable witness, or an exaggerated statement placed on the record. Unlike the Congress President who says "the public have not the time to verify intricate calculations, and they cannot be expected to follow the writer on Indian economics through the mazes of his figures, etc." (*vide* Mr. S. N. Bannerji's speech, page 22, Press copy). I am a great believer in figures. People who have "no time to verify intricate calculations" should not complain if thoughtful men decline to listen to them. When leaders of the Congress openly show their contempts for figures, how can they possibly expect the Government to accept their suggestions. No oratory can take the place of figures, and no "omnibus Resolutions" can disprove facts. I will quote chapter and verse for every statement I make. I am aware that there are some who are unwilling to believe anything written by English writers when dealing with Indian History, but every one must confess that no Mahomedan historian could be charged with inaccuracies, when recording events which happened under the Mahomedan Rulers, and which contains any reflection on their administration. I will therefore quote Mahomedan Historians—in some cases referring to the original Persian—to show how far Mr. Dutt was right in some of his statements, which history disproves. Mr. Dutt says that the Indian famines of the last quarter of the 19th Century have been unexampled in their intensity in the history of ancient and modern times. Let us see what Mahomedan Historians say; let us go back a thousand years and see what sort of famines visited us then.

The *Tarikh Badauni* says that about the year 960 A.D., a dreadful famine raged in the Eastern Provinces of Agra and Delhi. Even *Jawari* (barley) could not be obtained. Mahomedans and Hindus perished. Common people fed on the seeds of thorny acacia and on the hides of cattle. The famine was called *Khashmi Izad* (Wrath of God), which, according to the well-known Arabic *abjad* system of historical calculation gives the date. The author, Mulla Abdul Qadir, says that he witnessed with his own eyes men eating their own kind. Mulla Abdul Qadir is no obscure historian. He is mentioned in *Elphinstone's History of India* and *Biographical Dictionary*, L. U. K., etc. Mulla Abdul Qadir was a great scholar in Sanskrit also, and even now there are scholars who believe that *Rajtarangini* (the abriged history of Kashmir) was translated by Mulla Abdul Qadir and not by Maulana Imad-ud-din.

Tarikh Feruz Shahi, of Ziauddin Barni, is the chief source from which the great Ferishta draws his account of the period. This work says that in Jalaluddin's reign, about 1290 A.D., there was such a famine that "Hindus came into Delhi with their families twenty or thirty of them together, and in the extremity of hunger drowned themselves in the Jumna." The same historian says that in the reign of Sultan Mahomed "there was a fatal famine in Delhi and its environs, and throughout the Doab famine became general and continued for some years, and thousands perished; ryots were impoverished and reduced to beggary, lands were ruined, and cultivation was entirely arrested." The same Mahomedan historian refers to the great Malwa Famine about the same time. Delhi was devastated: "*not a thousandth part of the population remained*, the country was desolate and all cultivation abandoned, no horses and cattle were left in that part of the country." About the same time, in another part of the country, Barni says, "famine was so severe that man was devouring man." Referring to the Gujerat Famine in the same year *Tarikh Feruz Shahi* says "men and beasts died of starvation."

Zafarnamah, by Sharfuddin Yazdi (who died in 1446 A.D.), is an important historical work. This work, Mir Khond declares surpasses everything that had up to his time enlightened the world in the department of history. It is well known to the orientalists of Europe by the French translation of M. Petis de la Croix (*Histoire de Timur Bec*, Paris, 1722, 4 vols., 12mo), which is one of Gibbon's chief sources of information respecting that period. The French version was translated into English in 1723 by J. Darby. There is also an Italian translation by Bradutti. As all oriental scholars know, *Zafarnamah* is based on *Mulfizat-i-Timuri*; its translation into various European languages shows that it enjoys a high European reputation. An English translation of the *Zafarnamah* was published in the *Delhi Archæological Journal* in 1862, but I have not been able to find a copy. In *Zafarnamah* we find "women cutting in pieces and eating the skin of a horse which had been dead. Skins were boiled and sold in the markets. When bullocks were slaughtered, crowds rushed forward to catch the blood and consumed it for their sustenance."

It is admitted by every one that Akbar's reign was the best in the Mahomedan history of India. Let us see how the great Akbar fared as regards famine. Three great famines desolated the country during his reign. Abul Fazal Allami in his *Akbarnamah* refers to one of these thus:—"Men could not find corn; they were driven to the extremity of *eating each other, and some formed themselves into parties to carry off lone individuals for their food.*" The *Ain-i-Akbari* admits "at the time of famine and distress parents were allowed to sell their children."

Let another Mahomedan historian give his version of famine in Akbar's time: *Zubdat-ut-Tawarikh* was written by Shaikh Nurul Haq in the forty-second year of Akbar's reign, *viz.*, 1596 A.D. The third great famine in Akbar's reign, which took place only a year before the work was written, was a very severe one. "A fearful famine raged continuously for three or four years *throughout the whole of Hindustan*. A kind of plague also added to the horrors of this period and *depopulated whole cities*, to say nothing of hamlets and villages. In consequence of the dearth of grain and the necessities of *ravenous hunger, human flesh was eaten. The streets and roads were blocked up with dead bodies, and no assistance could be rendered for their removal."*

The italics are mine. I have given enough extracts to show how Upper India fared during a pre-British famine. I may now give an instance of famine in the Deccan. Mahomed Amin Kaziwini in his *Padshâhnamah* gives some harrowing details of a famine which raged about Daulatabad and Balaghat in the reign of Shah Jehan. We read "Inhabitants were reduced to the direst extremity. *Life was offered for a small loaf* (the original Persian is *Jáne-ba-náne*), *the ever bounteous hand was stretched out for food, dogs' flesh took the place of goats' flesh, and pounded bones of the dead was mixed with flour; destitution at length reached such a pitch that men began to devour each other, and the flesh of a son was preferred to his love."*

Tarikhi Tahiri was written in 1621 A.D. It gives an account of Sindh. The maulavies of Sindh consider it the best history of their country. The Amir of Khairapur and the Syeds of Thatta carefully preserve the *MSS.* of this work in their libraries. *Tarikhi Tahiri* says that there was such a famine in Sindh in the Fourteeth Century that a mother who could not see her sons perish before her eyes, besought them to kill her and satisfy the cravings of their hunger. The sons actually killed the mother.

Safarnamah Ibni Batutah, the *Muntakhabullubab* and *Mukhtasirat-Tawarikh*, and other well-known Persian works, give accounts of various famines in India. But I think I have given enough extracts from prominent Mahomedan historians.

Even making an allowance for Persian authors' *ibarati munshiana*—flowery and pedantic language, which European historians felicitously call the Jedediah Cleishbotham style—there is enough to prove beyond the shadow of doubt that famines in the pre-British period were much more *intense* than they have been in the last quarter of the Nineteenth Century. So, it is clear that Mr. Dutt has tripped, and tripped badly.

Even his friends are now coming forward to say that they

do not endorse all that Mr. Dutt says about famine. Mr. Pennington, I.C.S. (late Collector of Tanjore), who in *December, 1900* signed the memorable Petition addressed to the Secretary of State, in *December, 1902,* in public print says that he disagrees with Mr. Dutt in the alleged efficacy of a Permanent Settlement, and lays more stress on Irrigation. This is what Mr. Pennington says in an open letter to Mr. Dutt :—

"I do not know what exactly caused the famine in Bengal of 1770 as I have no books of reference here, though I fancy it was a good deal owing to war, unsettled Government, and over-assessment; but surely it is going too far to say that there has been no famine in Bengal *because* of the Permanent Settlement. There has certainly been no famine in Tanjore, Godavari, and Krishna since the work of Sir Arthur Cotton; yet there has been no Permanent Settlement. Nor is there any trace of famine in the Tambaraparni valley since the great irrigation works were carried out there some centuries ago, or in the Malabar and on the West Coast generally, where the climate is perhaps even more favourable than in Bengal. You yourself have said that famine is due primarily to failure of rain or of irrigation. Bengal is exceptionally well-watered, and like all irrigated districts, is practically safe against famine, *provided* it has a reasonable and settled Government and is not over-assessed. I cannot understand your saying 'that the Permanent Settlement has saved Bengal from the worst results of famines is proved by history as completely and unanswerably as any economic fact can be proved.' There seems to be no such proof at all."

When irrigation plays so important a part in averting famine and railways in mitigating its effects, let us see what the Government of India have done in these directions. An answer will be found in the following figures which give the expenditure on these two items from revenue.

Expenditure from Revenue in India on Railways and Irrigation, 1882-83 to 1897-98.

			Rs
1882-83	Railways	... ...	6,520,738
	Irrigation	... ...	2,480,912
			4,039,826
1883-84	Railways	... ...	6,808,186
	Irrigation	... ...	2,440,963
			4,367,223
1884-85	Railways	... ...	8,158,667
	Irrigation	... ...	2,501,949
			5,656,718
1885-86	Railways	... ...	8,975,159
	Irrigation	... ...	2,489,964
			6,485,195
1886-87	Railways	... ...	8,777,884
	Irrigation	... ...	2,416,712
			6,361,172
1887-88	Railways	... ...	9,068,422
	Irrigation	... ...	2,552,619
			6,515,803
1888-89	Railways	... ...	9,494,359
	Irrigation	... ...	2,692,950
			6,801,409

	Rs
1889-90—Railways	10,336,538
Irrigation	2,723,146
	7,613,392
1890-91—Railways	10,353,049
Irrigation	2,813,622
	7,539,427
1891-92—Railways	12,793,700
Irrigation	3,020,347
	9,773,353
1892-93—Railways	13,081,225
Irrigation	2,994,606
	10,086,619
1893-94—Railways	13,489,992
Irrigation	2,917,024
	10,572,968
1894-95—Railways	13,655,371
Irrigation	2,992,928
	10,662,443
1895-96—Railways	13,902,214
Irrigation	3,013,153
	10,889,061
1896-97—Railways	13,353,383
Irrigation	3,295,191
	10,058,192
1897-98—Railways	13,561,896
Irrigation	3,142,339
	10,419,557

The area under Irrigation in 1899-00 was 31,544,056 acres, and the area under crops 223,654,333. The following figures speak for themselves:—

Area under Irrigation in 1899-1900 in Acres.

Administration.	Total Area under Crops.	Area Irrigated.					
		By Canals.		By Tanks.	By Wells.	Other Sources.	Total Area Irrigated.
		Government.	Private.				
Bengal	65,708,800	754,577	...	...	...	...	754,577
N.W. Provinces ...	30,189,651	1,981,373	5,692	1,215,683	4,478,507	553,595	8,234,850
Oudh	11,413,508	...	...	976,394	1,643,178	80,453	2,700,025
Punjab	20,738,687	4,243,524	823,729	20,049	4,154,598	134,083	9,375,983
Lower Burma... ...	6,665,639	310	1,325	...	...	3,434	5,069
Upper Burma... ...	3,419,703	252,161	307,198	129,864	7,211	102,587	799,021
Central Provinces ...	17,043,937	...	810	176,187	64,188	14,079	255,264
Assam...	5,321,818	...	...	...	...	...	..
Ajmere-Merwara ...	394,844	...	...	7,228	43,776	116	51,120
Coorg	202,541	1,370	...	...	...	...	1,370
Madras	27,785,796	2,648,160	26,289	1,832,527	1,129,804	146,986	5,783,766
Bombay and Sind ...	27,975,223	2,452,262	145,608	30,443	698,794	188,563	3,515,670
Berar	6,787,318	...	72	...	66,638	107	67,070
Pergana Manpur ...	6,868	...	...	...	324	...	324
Total	223,654,333	12,333,737	1,310,723	4,388,375	12,287,218	1,224,003	31,544,056

The expenditure on Railways has also been shown and at the end of the year 1900 we had in India 24,707 miles of Railway thus:

	Miles.
Guaranteed Companies	1,305
Assisted Companies	1,514
State Lines	18,941
Native State Lines	2,873
Foreign Lines	74
Total ...	24,707

Mr. Dutt has referred to the "desolation" caused by famine. That thousands have fallen victims to want and disease, which tread close on the heels of a famine no one can deny, but the wonderfully recuperative power, which has asserted itself even after periods of prolonged drought, is amazing and counteracts the woeful effect of famine. Let me present a few figures—from the Province nearest to me—Bombay, during the *last quarter of the 19th Century,* which Mr. Dutt has singled out for his theme. What do we find? An increase in population in almost every district and a total increase in 20 years of 1,771,552. The figures of the last Census are of course excluded, because plague has raged for the past six years and nowhere more than in the Bombay Presidency, and their insertion would only vitiate the results.

Population of each district of the Bombay Presidency proper in 1872, *and* 1891.

Districts.	1872.	1891.
Ahmedabad	829,637	921,712
Kaira	782,733	871,589
Panch Mahals	240,743	313,417
Broach	350,322	341,490
Surat	607,087	998,949
Thana	847,424	819,580
Khandesh	1,028,642	1,460,851
Nasik	734,386	843,582
Ahmednagar	773,938	888,755
Poona	907,235	1,067,800
Sholapur	662,986	750,689
Satara	1,160,050	1,225,989
Belgaum	938,750	1,013,261
Dharwar	988,037	1,051,314
Bijapur	816,037	796,339
Kanara	398,406	446,351
Ratnagiri	1,019,136	1,105,926
Kolaba	350,405	594,872
Total ...	13,391,954	15,163,506

What effect the *famine of the last quarter of the 19th Century* (Mr. Dutt's words) had on the agriculture of the country and the agrarian population may be gathered from the following Table, which will show that the expression "desolation" used by Mr. Dutt must be taken in a quite modified sense.

Statement comparing the extent of fully assessed occupied area in Government Ryotwari and Khoti Villages in the Bombay Presidency during 1855-56, 1865-66, 1875-76 and 1895-96.

Districts.	1855-56.			1865-66.			1875-76.			1895-96.		
	No. of Government Village.	Occupied Area. Total.	Occupied Area. Average per Village.	No. of Government Village.	Occupied Area. Total.	Occupied Area. Average per Village.	No. of Government Village.	Occupied Area. Total.	Occupied Area. Average per Village.	No. of Government Village.	Occupied Area. Total.	Occupied Area. Average per Village.
1	2	3	4	5	6	7	8	9	10	11	12	13
NORTHERN DIVISION.												
Ahmedabad ...	499	325,503	652	459	496,993	1,083	443	500,217	1,129	447	493,455	1,104
Kaira ...	495	262,528	530	524	380,463	726	525	363,255	692	525	398,963	756
Panch-Mahal ...	...	...	...	457	(155,000)	(339)	435	152,388	350	403	220,072	551
Broach ...	406	403,719	994	406	453,613	1,117	410	466,811	1,139	407	469,565	1,154
Surat ...	807½	413,362	512	808	472,965	585	816½	584,239	716	810½	652,176	805
Thana ...	(2,216)	1,000.000	451	2,216	(1,000,000)	(451)	2,115	1,011,391	478	1,587	820,154	517
GENTRAL DIVISION.												
Khandesh ...	3,206½	1,294,644	404	3,853½	2,431,579	631	3,310½	2,415,638	730	2,704½	2,873,131	1,062
Nasik ...	...	...	...	...	...	...	1,508	1,821,840	1,208	1,500	2,025,257	1,350
Ahmednagar ...	1,879½	2,562,127	1,363	1,987½	3,507,794	1,765	1,215½	2,418,593	1,990	1,223½	2,552,989	2,087
Poona ...	970	1,447,006	1,492	1,561	3,481,723	2,230	990¾	1,875,670	1,893	1.002¾	1,898,179	1,893
Sholapur ...	917	1,962,895	2,141	...	...	...	660	2,147,432	3,254	665	2,071,770	3,115
Satara ...	1,180	1,428,086	1,210	1,020	1,651,568	1,619	959	1,421,055	1,482	961	1,397,714	1,454
SOUTHERN DIVISION.												
Belgaum ...	1,320	1,226,129	929	888	1,097,771	1,236	894	1,114,584	1,247	913	1,161,123	1,272
Bijapur ...	...	...	...	1,004	1,951,219	1,943	1,009	2,084,721	2,066	1,011	2,128,946	2,105
Dharwar ...	1,211	1,144,614	945	1,272	1,549,897	1,219	1,278	1,539,097	1,204	1,289	1,566,161	1,215
Kolaba ...	...	...	...	962½	412,715	428	985	468,646	475	1,538	689,255	448
Ratnagiri ...	1,279	(1,000,000)	782	1,277	(1,000,000)	(782)	1,273½	100,172	786	1,270½	1,624,002	1,278
Kanara ...	(1,416)	(320,000)	(226)	(1,416)	(320 000)	(226)	(1,416)	(320,000)	(226)	1,416	329,770	233
Total Presidency Proper ...	17,802½	14,790,613	831	20,111½	20,363,300	1,012	20,243¾	21,706,649	1,072	19,673¾	23,372,682	1,188

The area figures are for fully assessed occupied area. The figures in brackets are estimates only.

I have shown from Persian histories that Indian famines, before the advent of the British, affected *all classes,* because then famine meant *want of grain* whereas now it simply means *want of money* to buy grain. *Jawari* (a kind of barley), the poor man's staple food, sells in ordinary seasons at about 30 seers per rupee. The statistics relating to food grains show that during seasons of famine it never sold at less than 5 seers per rupee. In other words, in *extreme* cases the prices rose to about six times. Now let us see what happened a few centuries back before the English set foot in India. I have the authority of Mahomedan historians for stating that in pre-British famines the price of *Jawari,* which ordinarily sold at about 60 seers per rupee, rose to ½ seer per rupee, or in other words 120 times higher than the normal rates ! And we have also seen that often there was no grain to be had for any price, with the result that people had to live upon thorny acacia and cattle skin ! The famines of the *last quarter of the 19th Century* were not so intense, because they did not affect even the agricultural classes much. At all large relief works it as been found that the great majority of those seeking relief were not ryots but labourers. Evidently these had some means of support which helped them to tide over their temporary dfficulties. A glance at the Report of the Famine Commission of 1901 will show that here also I rely on the unimpeachablè testimony of figures. The famines in pre-British periods affected all classes, as is abundantly proved by history. Therefore, it is clear that *the famines of the 19th Century were not so intense as those that literally desolated the country before the British conquest of India.**

* The *Indian Review*, Madras, March, 1903.

AN ALIEN YOKE: OR—A DIVINE DISPENSATION?

> "There is a Divinity that shapes our ends,
> Rough hew them as you will."

I HAVE read with considerable interest Dr. Keene's article, "An Alien Yoke," in the last issue of the *Calcutta Review.* Dr. Keene says:—"*The pressure of taxation pure and simple only represents an average incidence of 1s. 10d. per head per annum.* * * * *Candour demands the admission that the alien yoke presses lightly on the Indians, and is not one which it can be their present interest to be rid.*"

But why should Dr. Keene calculate the "*present interest*" in £ s. d. only. What about other advantages? Is it an alien yoke or a Divine Dispensation?

The fundamental principle of all moral philosophy is that the real dignity of a man lies not in what he *has,* but in what he *is.* "The Kingdom of Heaven is within you." Such texts are no doubt to be found in the *Gita;* and Sākyamúni taught the ancient Hindus what Plato and Aristotle preached in the West, but it was left to England to show the degenerated *modern* Hindu the high ideal of human conduct and the earnestness of life. No doubt the wise Hippocrates 500 years before Christ said, "*Life is short, art long, opportunity fleeting, experiment slippery, judgment difficult,*" but it was the English who made the degenerated Hindus give up oddities, fribbles, and monstrosities, by giving them an idea of the real blood and bone of human heroism. The English, finding the degenerated Hindu as a sort of human lobster, who lived in the hard shell of "religious" crust, taught him the rarest of social virtues—moral courage. It is by coming in contact with the English that the *modern* Hindu eschewed his two besetting sins, moral cowardice and laziness. Punctuality and regularity he understands now; and, therefore, in the place of a hollow and worthless manhood, he enjoys a reasoned existence. Character—cultivated will—is better than lucre. This is England's gift to modern India. England has taught us that life is simply an energising reason, what Plato called the Imperial Mind is only another name of God. Crotchet-mongers and puzzle-brains will not agree with me, but I prefer the opinion of cool and practical thinkers. The battle of Plassey of 1757 was no doubt a decisive battle, but the great social and moral battles which England fights every day in India, imperceptibly shift the centre of gravity of modern Hindu social life. All the wisdom of the Greeks, all the learning of the Germans, could not have created such an atmosphere of pure and elevated sentiment which one finds nowadays in really educated and refined Indian society.

To understand properly what England has done for India, let us take a bird's-eye view of the main features of our history from the beginning of the last century. History is, or ought to be, a tracing of the causes which lead to successive events in the life story of a people. Accidents, pure and simple, are as rare in the history of a nation as they are in the life of an individual. Even when they do occur, they but cause a temporary aberration in the working of the great laws which regulate the march of events, and, having spent their forces, disappear, leaving the permanent and unalterable laws to work their way without further interruption. The facts of to-day are but the effects of those that preceded them. It is therefore necessary to know what happened before, in order to understand what is happening to-day.

Looking into the close of the 18th century we find Tipoo Sultan at the head of a powerful monarchy, viewing with no friendly eye the progress of a power that had just despoiled him of half his dominions. The Nizam, the Peshwa, the

Guikwar, the Raja of Nagpur, Holkar and Sindhia were as yet the sovereigns of large territories and the lords of immense armies, often trained by European officers. The Pindaris, all the turbulent spirits of the country focussed under the leadership of a number of soldiers of fortune, were scouring the country, leaving a track of blood and fire wherever they went. The Nawab Vazir of Oudh was busily engaged in consolidating his power in a province that his father had originally been sent out to govern. The Sikhs had just emerged from the grinding tyranny of a Muhammadan Governor, and were preparing to be a formidable power under the future Lion of the North. The Rajput princes had just succeeded in drowning the memory of Haldighat and Chitor under the stupefying influence of the "*Kusambha*." Descendants of Yashwant Singh and Mansingh had become the playthings of Amir Khan and the myrmidons of Sindhia and Holkar. Such were the princes who governed the country. Absolutism was the recognised form of Government. Almost all these Governments had their origin within the memory of men then living, and which they owed to the successful rapacity of some powerful soldier or other, whose successors had not forgotten the origin of their power and were fully bent upon maintaining it by the same instrument with which they had been acquired. They were ever intriguing for each others' destruction, and had consequently no time to look to the internal administration of their dominions. The requirements of their large armies forced them to raise as much money as they could amongst their subjects; hence from their point of view their fiscal administration was always well organised. But the other portions of their administration were always in a deplorable state; there were practically no courts of record in their dominions; Judgeships in their civil courts were either openly auctioned, or given to court favourites without any regard to the qualifications of the candidates. Smaller criminal offences were seldom enquired into by anyone, except the "Kotwal" (Police Commissioner) who generally coverted them into a source of revenue for himself. Almost every article of commerce constituted the subject of a private monopoly conferred upon a favourite wife or a boon companion. The princes sometimes had their private trading establishments and banks, where people were forced to buy and sell at prices fixed by their rulers. The farmers of revenue were nominally responsible for the Police Administration of their villages, but as a matter of fact every strong man could do whatever he chose. Brute force was the only principle recognised by these fortune's playthings for the hour; success amongst them justified all enormities; honesty had ceased to guide their public relations; treaty engagements were entered into only to be broken at the first opportunity; assassination of an enemy, either by poison or the dagger, did not raise horror in a single breast and the sacred ties of kinship were broken with perfect impunity. Amongst their subjects the exactions of Government and the scanty protection afforded to them against foreign invasions and internal robberies, the want of roads, and the utter want of protection thereon, the numerous tolls, and other dues they were called upon to pay, struck at the root of honest industry, and transformed many an honest agriculturist or trader into a robber and a cut-throat. Violence and rapine were the only things that prospered in this unnatural state of society.

There was, however, one portion of the continent which was free from this state of anarchy and confusion. The Company's dominions on the eastern coast and about Bombay, amidst all this universal discordance and confusion enjoyed tranquility. They were free from invasions from without, and, in spite of great imperfections in almost every branch of the then existing administration, there was much greater security of life and property to be found in them than anywhere else on the continent. Decennial Settlement had given an impetus to agriculture that was previously unknown in the country. The summary execution of dacoits (robbers) at the scenes of their crimes made the roads free for the purposes of trade. The Company's trade opened a fresh market for the produce of the country. The result was that numbers of merchants from the Native States came and settled near the Company's factories in order to profit by security and justice which prevailed there. Whilst of the poorer sort, large numbers took service in the

Company's army for the pay and pension it held out to them. These on their return home spread most favourable reports of the Company's Government. This comparative excellence of the Company's administration contained within itself the key to the seemingly paradoxical fact of the conquest of an enormous country by a handful of the factory servants of a trading Company. Never in the history of the world has such an enormous result been accomplished with such slender means. Even Peru and Mexico required more men and ampler means to conquer them. The question naturally arises "What was the cause of this extraordinary phenomenon?" Patriotic Englishmen good humouredly attribute it to the superior stamina of the Anglo-Saxon race, and gravely assure us that "India was conquered by the sword." But such of their countrymen as read and think, know, that though gratifying to the national feeling, the explanation is inconsistent with fact and opposed to probabilities. A reference to history will show, even to the most careless reader, that in almost every battle fought by Englishmen in India five-sixths at least of the conquering army consisted of unmixed Indians. *The absolute want of faith in their own Government could alone have produced such a result.* Sir David Barr in his paper "Akbar: or—Victoria?" very rightly observes: "Overwhelming force of arms will *conquer* a country, or seize an empire; but it *requires conciliation* to weld the conquest, to bring the conquered nation into subjection and to give root to the administration." We have seen above how, on the dismemberment of the Moghul empire, the country had become a prey to hostile factions; how the different families which had assumed to themselves regal power had failed to win the affections of their people and had become positively hateful to them by the enormity of their crimes, the ferocity of their exactions, and the insufficient protection which they afforded. Amongst a people with a better political history, this state of things would very likely have resulted in a domestic revolution followed by the establishment of limited monarchies or republics. But a Government evolved out of the wishes of the people was a thing unknown to India. Implicit obedience to the ruling power was alike inculcated by religion and precedent, and the people passively wished for the advent of a better and a stronger power. The East India Company was such a power.

Referring to their despatches of the earlier part of the last century we find the Court of Directors repeatedly warning their Governors against any further territorial aggrandisement, nay, sometimes recalling such Governors for disobedience of their orders on this point. Yet we find, in spite of this repeated warning and prospective dismissal, each successive governor entering into fresh wars which always ended in the "much deprecated territorial aggrandisement." The new governors came out with a sincere desire to be on terms of friendship with the neighbouring princes, and yet no sooner had they landed in the country than they found themselves embroiled in wars. The fact was that the Indian Government was such that a State was compelled either to attack and cripple, if not altogether extinguish its neighbours, or allow itself to be extinguished. Possessing the requisite strength themselves, and knowing the weakness of their neighbours, the Company's Governors naturally preferred the former course. They soon learnt that in India safety meant supremacy, and as they naturally loved the first, they found themselves forced to seek it by securing the latter. This supremacy was practically attained about the close of the Second Mahratta War. The policy of forcing the Native Governments to keep armies officered by Englishmen, pursued by the Marquis of Wellesley, put an end to the ever-recurring broils that had made existence a burden and improvement an impossibility. With this change in the position of the Government we find a marked change in its policy. This was the period of peaceful improvements.

Lord Minto in 1811 wrote:

"It is a common remark that science and literature are in a progressive state of decay among the natives of India. From every enquiry which I have been enabled to make on this interesting subject, that remark appears to me but too well-founded. The number of the learned is not only diminished, but the circle of learning, even amongst those who still devote themselves to it, appears to be considerably contracted. The abstract sciences are abandoned, polite literature neglected, and no branch of learning cultivated but what is connected with the peculiar religious doctrines of the people. The immediate consequence of this state of things is the disuse and even actual loss of many books, and it is to be apprehended that unless Government interpose with a fostering hand, the revival of letters may shortly become hopeless, from a want of books or of persons capable of explaining them."

In 1813 the East India Company directed: "That a sum of not less than a lakh of rupees in each year shall be set apart, and applied to the revival and improvement of literature, and the encouragement of the learned natives of India and for the introduction and promotion of a knowledge of the sciences among the British territories of India."

The first English newspaper in India was *Hickey's Gazette*, started in 1780. The next paper was the *Bengal Journal*. The Editor of the *Bengal Journal*, Mr. William Duane, was deported from India in 1794. The next paper of any importance was the *Calcutta Journal*, but in 1823 the editors, Messrs. Buckingham and Sandfort Arnot, were deported from India for writing scurrilous articles against Dr. Bryce, a high official of the Government.

The immolation of widows was made penal in 1829. The Regulation of 4th December, 1829, is a memorable document: "It is hereby declared, that after the promulgation of this Regulation, all persons convicted of aiding and abetting in the sacrifice of a Hindu widow by burning or burying her alive, *whether the sacrifice be voluntary on her part or not*, shall be deemed guilty of culpable homicide, and shall be liable to punishment by fine or imprisonment or both by fine and imprisonment."

A Registration Act and a quantity of adjective law on miscellaneous subjects under the name of "constructions" were promulgated. Post Offices were established throughout the country; each district was subdivided into a number of Thanahs presided over by a Darogha, Schools and Colleges were opened for the benefit of the people; the memorable controversy about the expediency of imparting education through the medium of English or the Indian vernaculars, was settled happily in favour of the former. In 1835 Lord Macaulay wrote: "I think it clear that we are not fettered by any pledge expressed or implied; that we are free to employ our funds as we choose, that we ought to employ them to teaching what is best worth knowing; that English is better worth knowing than Sanskrit or Arabic; that the natives are desirous to be taught English, and are not desirous to be taught Sanskrit or Arabic; that neither as the language of law nor as the language of religion have the Sanskrit and Arabic any peculiar claim to our encouragement; *that it is possible to make natives of this country thoroughly good English scholars, and that to this end our efforts ought to be directed.*"

The language difficulty was thus overcome. The great complexity and variety of the Indian vernaculars is well summed up by Dr. Grierson:—

"There are languages whose phonetic rules prohibit the existence of more than a few hundred words, which cannot express what to us are the commonest and most simple ideas; and there are others with opulent vocabularies, *rivalling English in their copiousness and in their accuracy of idea-consolidation.* There are languages, every word of which must be a monosyllable, and others in which syllable is piled on syllable till the word is almost a sentence by itself. There are languages which know neither noun nor verb, and whose only grammatical feature is syntax, and others with grammatical systems as complicated as those of Greek and Latin. There are parts of India which recall the plain in the land of Shinar where the tower of old was built, and in which almost each of the many mountains had its own language, and there are great plains, tens of thousands of miles in area, over which one language is spoken from end to end."

In 1833 the following order was issued:

"And be it enacted that no native of the said territories, nor any natural born subject of His Majesty resident therein, shall by reason only of his religion, place of birth, descent, colour, or any of them, be disabled from holding any place, office, or employment, under the said Company." Natives of India were then, for the first time, employed by the British authorities in offices of trust and responsibility.

Lord Dalhousie incorporated into the Empire the dominions of the princes of Nagpur, Jhansi, Coorg, and Lucknow, the first three on the ground of intestacy, and the last on that of mal-administration. The Punjab was also annexed. These annexations resulted in the benefit of the subject, and every lover of human liberty must rejoice that personal government in them was displaced by government by law. The Marquis went home and was succeeded by Lord Canning. The peace-loving character of the new Viceroy, the prosperous state of the country, the strength of the army, and the efficiency of the Civil Service, everything combined to promise a glorious and peaceful reign. But a shock was soon felt throughout the Empire in the unexpected mutiny of the Bengal Army. It will be beyond the scope of this article to trace the causes or the course of that national calamity. We will therefore pass over it and proceed to examine the manners and customs of the people of those times, their education, habits of thought, religion and superstition. These will give us a clear idea of the improvements made since.

The residence of a Hindu gentleman, of Bengal for instance, of the pre-mutiny period, generally consisted of three sets of buildings round as many contiguous quadrangles. The first was his "*kutcherry*" (the office), the second his place of worship and festivities, and the third his zenana (female apartments). He got up between 4 and 5 A.M., told his beads for about an hour, then sat in his "*kutcherry*" till about 10 A.M., disposing of disputes amongst his tenantry, examining his accounts, consulting astrologers, dictating letters, and deciding caste questions. He then bathed and worshipped his family idols till about noon and took his meals. Then after making some enquiries about the arrangement for his guests, he retired for an hour or so, got up between 3 and 4 P.M. and held his "*kutcherry*" till sunset. His evenings were spent either in listening to the recital of the Puranas by a priest or to music, of which generally he was a fairly good judge. He kept an open house where every stranger could find food and shelter for the asking. His food consisted principally of rice, flour, pulses, fruits, vegetables, milk, ghee (clarified butter), and sugar. His education consisted in some knowledge of Persian imparted to him early in his life, but which he never took the trouble to revise, a smattering of Sanskrit (if he was a Brahman), and a decent acquaintance with his own vernacular. His arithmetic reached up to what we now call "practice." Of history he knew only the fables of the Puranas and of the Shahnamah, his geography seldom extended beyond the limits of his own district. He believed in ghosts and demons, witches and incantations; a priest was regularly employed in his house to read some sacred book or other to invoke the aid of the gods in warding off the evils of destiny. He had an unlimited contempt for all foreigners except perhaps Englishmen. He felt honoured in shaking hands with an Englishman but never forgot to bathe and purify himself to expiate for the pollution! He was simple, quiet and courteous in his manner, and inexpensive in his habits. He was charitable to a fault, and religious according to his own idea of religion. A widow marriage, or the partaking of prohibited food scandalized him beyond all measure; but he could tolerate a bribe-taking official or a lying neighbour. He discarded his only son for marrying out of his caste, but did not scruple to win a contested lawsuit with the assistance of documents of questionable authenticity backed by mendacious witnesses. Such were the country gentlemen of the pre-mutiny period. The common people were more superstitious and ignorant; scarcely one in ten thousand could write his own name. Almost all of them worked as agriculturists, some on their own farms, others as farm servants. Domestic service or the dangerous calling of club-men (*lathials*) were the only other alternatives offered them by the then society. They were still barefooted, and what was worse, almost naked and decidedly poor. The growing demands of an increasing population and an ever widening export trade had, it is true, raised both rent and prices, but the cultivator received but a small share of the increase. As yet there was no fixity of tenure in land and the sharp competition of an ever-increasing tenantry made the *malguzar* (land owner) the master of the field.

The educated classes were as yet few in number and of very little influence in the country. In the more important towns the schools and colleges had begun a silent revolution which has ever been at work since then, and of which the end is not yet visible to any of us. Government had wisely prohibited the teaching of any particular religion in its institutions. But the introduction of Physical Science and of Inductive Philosophy into the College curriculum did more to shake the student's belief in the old faith than if Paley and Butler had been part of the prescribed course. The missionaries headed by men like Carey, Duff, Marshman, and other eminent scholars, made converts of some of the most promising young men of the most advanced Province of India—Bengal ; and the faith of the rest was rudely shaken. The Hindu priests of the period, steeped to the lips in the fantastic and unreasoned stories of the Purans, appealed to their authority, which the young men despised. The emancipated children of a priest-ridden country rose in open rebellion against the old religion, which they threatened to tear up root and branch. Under the rebound, the distinction between a crafty priesthood and a pure religion was forgotten. The young men took pride in openly doing everything which the old religion had prohibited. It was the old story of the pendulous folly of mankind having gone the other way. For a time, an educated Hindu correlated the idea of hard drinking and meat eating; and disregard of Hindu feelings, even in indifferent matters, came to be regarded as necessary ingredients in the formation of an educated Hindu. But the country was soon relieved from this state of godless profligacy by the appearance of Brahma leaders who, discarding the untenable dogmatism of the later Puranas, went deep into the Vedas and evolved pure Theism out of them. They were surrounded by all the purer spirits of the time, and the Brahmaism of the old school henceforth became practically the dominant faith of the educated classes. These men established societies and published books and articles for the reform of social abuses. It was mainly through their exertions that the Civil Marriage Act was passed. Pandit Ishwar Chandra Vidyasagar took an active part. The Brahmas preached anathemas against infant marriage, exposed the follies and crimes of the priestly class, and entered into religious controversies with the missionaries of the time.

As yet there were perhaps no more than a dozen newspapers in the country. Nearly half of these were English, and with the exception of one, were conducted by Europeans. Gradually vernacular papers were started. They were mostly filled with local news and gossip, and contained very little worth reading. Economics or politics seldom received any attention at their hands, and there was as yet no arrangement for press telegrams from Europe or America. The papers were mostly in the hands of uneducated people, and were filled up with "humorous" and satirical and sometimes obscene articles against the missionaries, and whatever of public or private nature that occurred in the town whence they emanated.

As yet the P. and O. Company had not made the passage to England short. There was no such large body of non-official Europeans in the country as now. Years rolled over them in their District or Sub-Divisions without their seeing a single European. Their situation forced them either to remain altogether isolated or to mix with the people. Even the most reserved chose the latter. They attended the festivals of the people, were honoured guests at their marriages and funerals, attended *nautch* (Native Dance) parties, organised wrestling matches and horse races, and taught young men to shoot and hunt in their company. There being no railways, nor refreshment rooms at the time, they often had to thank a hospitable landlord or *mahājan* (banker) for a few "*Chapatis*" (Indian bread) and a night's rest. On the other hand, there was as yet no aspiration on the part of the governed to stand on equal terms with their governors, and no Ilbert Bill or Local Self-government Act to disturb the harmonious relations between them. *The relationship was one between a patron and his protégé.*

The Mutiny had passed over the country like a thunderstorm, and like all such phenomena had left the political atmosphere much clearer than before. Thousands of families mourned the loss of dear relatives or of large fortunes; but those who survived obtained the Queen's Proclamation of 1858 granting special privileges to all subjects, irrespective of colour and creed, race and domicile. Sir C. Wood's despatch of 1854 was given effect to, by the establishment of three Universities at the three Presidency towns with a number of colleges affiliated to each. Two Lieutenant-Governorships were created for the better administration of the Bengal Presidency. A general and three local Legislatures were established to frame laws for the varying requirements of a progressive society. A High Court of Justice was established at each Presidency town with better defined powers, in the place of the old Supreme Courts. New railways were opened, telegraphs laid, and feeder roads constructed for the better carriage of traffic; steamers took the place of the old sailing vessels, and a keen competition amongst independent European merchant firms replaced the practically monopolous trade of the East India Company. A Civil and Criminal Procedure Code, a Limitation Act and a Penal Code were passed, besides a number of local Acts in the place of the old "constructions" and the Mahomedan Criminal Law. These were amongst the beneficial measures that immediately succeeded the transfer of the Government from the Company to the Crown. Since then we have had Municipalities and Local Funds established for the administration of local affairs, and natives of India introduced into them, at first—as was only proper—cautiously; when it was found that the experiment succeeded, Indians sometimes obtained at the hands of Government almost the same privileges in these respects as were enjoyed by the people of England. More than one Hindu has acted as Chief Justice, and two Bengalis having given satisfaction as Divisional Commissioners, one has been appointed member of the Board of Revenue in Bengal. Indians have been extensively employed in the service of the Government in almost every branch of the Civil administration. Mass Education, Economic Museums, well digested

Rent Laws, and Department of Agriculture and Commerce—in short every act of Government is marked by a liberality of spirit and a wise policy seldom displayed by a foreign Government in the administration of a conquered country.

In the year of the opening of the Universities, hundreds of students went in for the Matriculation Examination. Enterprising and well-to-do young men, disregarding the anathema of caste, ventured the peril of the sea and entered the Indian Civil Service through the broad door of competition. The Government of Sir John Lawrence, to show its appreciation of this bold departure, opened a number of scholarships to compensate young Indians for the extra hardships they were put to, in competing for the service. A number of young men went to Europe. Indian merchants went to England on business; gentlemen at large began to visit the British Isles for pleasure and instruction. These men returned home deeply imbued with the spirit of the institutions of the country of their sojourn. They were met half way by the educated classes at home. Numbers of educated men had entered the Uncovenanted Services of Government as Munsifs, Sub-Judges, Deputy Magistrates, Surgeons, Engineers, and Deputy Collectors; others again had joined the Bar or had taken to trade. Most of these men came from the middle classes; some belonged to its upper strata. But as intellect is practically the only recognised force in modern society, the origin of these men was soon forgotten in their power. In India there scarcely was any aristocracy save that of service. The proudest Indian Noble is forced to admit that the founder of his family was a successful Government servant. These new men were in the same position, and it was only natural that they commanded the same influence. Newspapers were started on all sides both in English and in vernaculars containing selections from English papers of the speeches of public men of England, replete with criticism of the measures of Government as would be tolerated only in England or America. These made a deep impression on the minds of the people. The party organisation of England furnished them with a ready model for forming associations like the *British Indian* (Calcutta), the *Sarvajanika* (Poona), and the *Anjuman* (Madras). To some there was nothing astonishing that the new generation should think more of their present rights than of their past history. The ideal Government which they had been taught to value, required that a nation should tax itself; that beneficial legislation is impossible except by a representative assembly; that the people should have some control over the national expenditure. The correctness of these *abstract* propositions was never doubted by any thoughtful man in England within the last century; young India—like the inexperienced person that he was—asserted that what is sauce for the goose must also be sauce for the gander. He forgot that there was another side of the picture, another point of light from which the case may be viewed. The average Englishman naturally looked with anger and disgust on what seemed to him the saucy ingratitude of a people who, only a century ago, were practically slaves under the Muhammadan Government, and who owed to himself almost everything that made life desirable—its education, security, and a good deal of its possessions—claiming equal rights with himself. He belonged to a privileged class and his privileges were being attacked, he could not easily realize that a people to whom the fundamental principles of Government had been almost unknown only half a century ago should claim to govern itself, nay, openly assert that they could do it better and cheaper. It was true that he had taken pity on an intelligent race, made a foster child of it, given it a liberal education; had filled it with rapturous admiration with his account of the chivalrous resistance of Hampden or the disinterested patriotism of Washington, Mazzini, and Garibaldi. He had taken it behind the screen to look into the origin of Governments under the guidance of Bentham, Lubbock, and Maine, he had sent him to Austin, Hallam, Amos, and May to learn the conditions under which a Government is entitled to claim obedience at the hands of the subject—the Englishman had done all this for the Indian. But he had never thought that his protégé would try to embody his idealism into facts, and that at so short a notice. It was the case of the fond parent feeling hurt at the assertion of a will of its own by the child for whom he had done so much.

Matters were at this stage when Lord Lytton assumed the reins of Government. His Lordship passed the Press Act and opened the Statutory Service. He was succeeded by Lord Ripon who passed the Local Self-Government Act and repealed the Press Act. But the further progress of his policy was checked by the unfortunate introduction of the Ilbert Bill. It was a measure not at all calculated to do any real good to the subject race, and touched a vital point of privilege of the ruling class. In politics much must be surrendered to expediency, specially when the Indian from time immemorial has been used to inequality in laws. Mr. R. C. Dutt, C.I.E., in "*Civilization in Ancient India*" says :—"There was one law for the Brahman, another for the Sudra ; the former was treated with undue leniency, the latter with *excessive and cruel severity.* If a Brahman committed one of the four or five heinous crimes enumerated in the law-books, *i.e.*, if he slew a Brahman, violated his guru's (religious teacher) bed, stole the gold of a Brahman, or drank spirituous liquor, the King branded him on the forehead with a heated iron and banished him from his realm. If a man of lower caste slew a Brahman he was punished with death and the confiscation of his property. If such a man slew a man of equal or lower caste, other suitable punishments were meted out to him (Baudhāyana I, 10, 18 and 19)." Admitting that it was only a prejudice of the ruling race, the subject race should even then have respected it as it really entailed no hardship on them. In the end they were beaten on the point, and much valuable time that could have been better utilized was lost on it. A good deal of race antipathy was evolved out of it, and it entailed some personal suffering on individuals.

For the last fifty years the whole of India has had but one literature for its educated classes. Every educated man has gone through practically the same studies, has had his ideas and tastes formed by the same authors, and has been affected by the same laws and by the same system of Government. The Railway, the Telegraph and the Steamer Service have in a great measure brought the most distant parts of the country near one another. The Calcutta lawyer now spends his *Dussera* in Bombay and Poona, and the Madras Chetty his Christmas holidays in Calcutta and Bombay. The exigencies of the Imperial Service, and of an extensive and ever increasing internal trade bring the people of the different parts of the country into daily contact. The spirit for travel, that the Indians have imbibed from their conquerors, now permeates through every stratum of society; even students now spend their college recesses in visiting distant parts of the country. Fifty years ago the presence of a Maharatta turban would have collected a jeering crowd in the streets of Calcutta, the Honourable Mr. Gokhale now drives undisturbed through the same streets, except it be when he returns a friendly greeting. The absence of all religious teaching from the educational institutions has added a motive to unity. It is no longer an uncommon sight to see a dozen men from different parts of the country and belonging to different castes sitting down together to a friendly dinner. Cases may be quoted of inter-marriages between inhabitants of different Provinces of the Empire. Personal contact daily points out to them unmistakable evidence of a common origin in more or less the same manners and customs prevailing amongst all of them. Thus, of the factors which constitute nationality—a common origin, a single government, and a common literature—two are the direct gifts of England to India, and the other has also been more vividly brought before us through her instrumentality. It will yet take the Indians a great many years to be a compact and united people, but under the protection of the British Government, the soldering has begun is a proposition that can admit of no doubt.

The first thing that strikes one is the gradual disruption of the Hindu family system. The "Karta" (Head of the family) is daily losing ground, and individual will is fast becoming predominant. People now shift for themselves as soon as they are able to earn an independent livelihood; the sight of an entire family of able-bodied men consuming in idleness the fruits of one man's labour does not so often offend the eye. It is to be hoped that the golden mean in this respect will not be overstepped, and a loving regard and a spirit ever-ready to assist one's relatives in their hour of need will not forsake the natives of India.

Female education is making rapid progress in the country. Wherever there is a large intellectual class may be found a number of well-educated ladies. The University authorities have allowed ladies to compete for degrees on equal terms with men, and at present we can count the number of Hindu lady graduates by the dozen. The demand for educated wives increases every year and the supply is also fast on the increase. In India, women now enjoy more consideration and greater liberty than they used to do fifty years ago. The really educated Hindu now understands that it is a suicidal policy to lock up half the race. By coming in contact with Englishmen he now clearly sees that "the hand which rocks the cradle rules the world." He now allows the ladies of his family to escape from the ancient restrictions of superannuated customs, and adorn and delight wider circles than domestic surroundings. He has now confidence in female virtue, and is convinced that the educated Hindu lady of to-day may safely be given the liberty which her ancestors enjoyed in ancient India. To some of the Bengali ladies of to-day, even Herbert Spencer and John Stuart Mill are no strangers; they read Victor Hugo's poems and Moliere's dramas. They now, with ease, follow the upward march of their husbands, and are quite fitted to take a high place in any society. The refined Indian lady is not the result of violent or hasty reform. The reform commenced with Raja Ram Mohan Roy in 1813. In connection with female education in India, the names of Lady Amherst and Miss Cook (1819) will always be remembered with gratitude. They were the pioneers of female education in Bengal. Thirty years later, on the 7th May, 1849, the Bethune School was opened for the education of Bengali girls. The Brahma Samaj has done a great deal in this direction. In 1866 Bengali ladies first appeared in public. It was during the Māghotsab of that year that a Bengali lady (Mrs. S. N. Tagore) appeared in an evening party in the Government House, Calcutta. A great deal has been accomplished within the last forty years towards the amelioration of the condition of women in India, but much remains yet to be done.

The last Census shows improvement in almost every direction. Sir Charles Elliott, late Lieutenant-Governor of Bengal, says that the Census of 1901 clearly shows a vast increase in the population of India from 205 to 294 millions in thirty years. Another hopeful sign, writes Sir Charles Elliott, is that progress in learning English is far more rapid than the spread of general education. In 1891 the number who had learnt the language of the conquering race was returned as 537,811, or 36 males and 5 females in every 10,000. Now the total number is 1,125,231 persons, or 68 males and 7 females in every 10,000. The largest number of English literates is found in Bengal, where they number 370,000; Madras comes next with 190,000 and Bombay with 144,000. No other province reaches 100,000. It is unfortunate, however, that the Census Report does not distinguish the English and Eurasians, who learn English instinctively, from the native population who learn it educationally, as a foreign language. In 1891 out of the total figure of 537,811 the native element counted for 386,032. Assuming that a similar proportion obtains now, *the number of natives who have learnt English would be about 789,000, or double what it was in 1891.*

The number returned as literate in all India is 15,686,421, or 53 per *mille* of the entire population. Of these 14,690,080 are males, and only 996,341 are females, or 98 per thousand among males and 7 among a thousand females. The province which holds the highest place in respect to literacy is Burma; for 378 per thousand of its male population and 45 per thousand of its females can read and write. This is due to the wide-spread system of free education imparted by the Buddhist Monks at the monasteries, at which it is customary for every male Burman child to spend at least a year, while the instruction of females is not hampered by the prejudices in favour of their seclusion when they approach the age of puberty, which so greatly impede progress in other parts of India.

The highest authorities in the country have pronounced their judgments in favour of the honesty of native officers in the Judicial Service. Untruth and want of candour are now as much deprecated in educated Indian society as they are among Englishmen. A high authority once wrote in a public document that the really educated native is more English than the average Englishman. That may be an exaggeration, but there can be no doubt that with their progress in education the Indians have become more honest, truthful and candid in all their relations. Public spirit, in the western sense, was a thing almost unknown fifty years ago. Now there are people who are prepared to lose a great deal in their endeavours for the public good. Fifty years ago to be accused of cowardice, moral or physical, was scarcely considered an insult, and physical weakness was not looked upon as a misfortune. The case is very different now. Those who read newspapers with a view to mark the changes that are taking place around us, cannot fail to notice that a spirit of resistance to personal aggression has already arisen. There is now scarcely a college in the country which has not its gymnasium. Purely Indian circuses attract the admiration of Europeans, and gentlemen athletes are not uncommon.

The English conquest of India has made it possible for the occident and orient to meet. The result is that both are benefitted. Orthodox Hindus who pretend to dislike everything English in reality *admire* everything English. This may seem paradoxical. But it is true. Erudite Indian scholars like Taranath Tarakavāchaspati and Bharat Chandra Siromani did not receive a tenth of the homage that Pandit Ishwar Chandra Vidyasagar and Swami Vivekānanda did. In oriental learning, all Bengal will admit Tarakavāchaspati and Siromani were much superior to Vidyasāgar and Vivekānanda. Vidyasagar and Vivekānanda's knowledge of English helped them to compare Hindu philosophy with western thought. Hence their fame. Take another example, Bankim Chandra Chatterji, the great Bengali writer. His *Dharmatatva* is practically Mill's philosophy in oriental garb. His Bhagvat-Gita is a great favourite in Bengal, because in its pages views of western savants like Lassen and Weber are discussed.

India must learn western ways and keep pace with the west or she must go to the wall. Sir David Barr in his article on "Victoria" very pertinently observes, "the primary difficulty in India, no matter how worthy the object, is the apathy of those who should be most interested in the welfare of the country. There is no gainsaying the fact that a desire for united action for the common weal is not one of the attributes of the people of India." India must *assimilate* western ways. Blind *imitation* will not do. The Indian must try to harmonize Eastern practices with Western Civilisation. India under England has *gained* a great deal and likely to gain more. British supremacy in India, therefore, instead of being an *alien yoke*, is really a *Divine Dispensation*.*

* The *Calcutta Review*, January, 1905.